Christopher Howard's
Guide to
Costa Rican Spanish

D0886186

Developed by Costa Rica Books, S.A.
and Astro Enterprises, Panama

© 2010 Costa Rica Books/
Astro Enterprises, Panama

COSTA RICA BOOKS
Suite 1 SJO 981
P.O. Box 025216
Miami, FL 33102-5216
Toll-free 800-365-2342 or 877-884-2502
E-mail: christopher@costaricabooks.com

ISBN 10: 1-881233-87-1
ISBN 13: 978-1-881233-87-9

Printed in China
Impreso en China

ABOUT THE AUTHOR

Christopher Howard has lived in Costa Rica for over thirty years and is a Costa Rican citizen.

He has an extensive foreign language background, having earned a B.A. in Latin American studies and a Master's degree in Spanish from the University of California. In addition to this, he has credentials to teach Spanish at all levels from California State University, San Francisco.

He was the recipient of scholarships for graduate study at the University of the Americas in Puebla, Mexico and the Jesuit University of Guadalajara, Mexico in conjunction with the University of San Diego, California. He has written three foreign language books, including the original Costa Rican Spanish Survival Course, and in 1985 he founded a successful language institute in San José, Costa Rica.

Mr. Howard has had the opportunity to do extensive research in the field of the Spanish language while living in Costa Rica. When he first came to the country, he became fascinated by the way the Costa Ricans spoke their particular style of Spanish. Although he had an excellent foundation in Spanish, it proved difficult to understand the locals. Consequently, the author began to dissect the local language and all of its nuances. The collection of expressions in this book is the result of Mr. Howard's efforts and research. Their is no other source of this information in English.

At present, the author writes the columns, "Learning the Language" for the Association of Residents of Costa Rica's (ARCR) magazine *La Voz*, "Learn Spanish" for *Inside Costa Rica* and "Spanish Tips" for *Costa Rica Living* and for *AM Costa Rica*.

Due to his expertise, Christopher Howard is frequently called on to give seminars on the subject of learning Spanish as a foreign language. He can be found lecturing at the Association of Residents of Costa Rica's monthly seminar for newcomers.

Mr. Howard has also worked as a paid consultant for *National Geographic Magazine* and published numerous articles for newsletters about living in Costa Rica and the rest of Central America. He has written 16 editions the perennial best-selling "New Golden Door to Retirement and Living in Costa Rica," the popular "Guide to Real Estate in Costa Rica" and guidebooks about Panama, Nicaragua, Mexico and Cuba.

Finally, since 1997 Christopher Howard has conducted one-of-a-kind monthly relocation and retirement tours to Costa Rica. Through his monthly tours, seminars, and private consultation services, he has personally introduced thousands of people to Costa Rica.

- The Publisher

INTRODUCTION

Although many of Costa Rica's well-educated people speak English (and more than 50,000 English-speaking foreigners live permanently in Costa Rica), Spanish is the official language. So anyone who seriously plans to live or retire in Costa Rica should know some Spanish—the more the better.

Part of the fun of living in another country is communicating with the local people, making new friends, and enjoying the culture. Speaking Spanish will enable you to achieve these ends, opening the door for many new, interesting experiences.

Most English speakers who come to Costa Rica will find it hard to understand and communicate with the locals. Even people who speak Spanish can have a difficult time with the local slang. Like English, Spanish is very idiomatic. In Costa Rica, everyday conversations are filled with local jargon called *tiquismos*.

The result of twenty years of experience, experimentation, and research in the field of bilingual education, this guide will help you decipher most of the local idioms in Costa Rica and enable you to communicate on a basic level. Tiresome grammar and tedious exercises have been eliminated both to accelerate and facilitate the learning process and make this book more enjoyable. Thus, people of all ages and from all walks of life can profit from it.

This is not, however, a complete course in the Spanish language. But with the regular practice of the pronunciation exercises and memorization of all the indispensable vocabulary and useful phrases, you should be able to communicate and handle most daily situations you will encounter in Costa Rica.

Remember what Cervantes said: "To know another language is to know another world."

Good Luck! ¡Buena Suerte!

CONTENTS

Part I
Simple Pronunciation Guide

A. In pronouncing Spanish vowel sounds, the jaw, lips, and tongue muscles are held steadier than in English. With plenty of practice, you can sound like a Spanish speaker.

IMPORTANT NOTE: In part II entitled "Spanish Survival Phrases for Daily Situations", there is NO pronunciation guide before or after the words and phrases as in other pocket Spanish guidebooks of this type.

By mastering the simple rules and basic vowel sounds below there is NO need for a phonetic pronunciation guide. This way you will not be dependent on a guide as a crutch and should be able to pronounce words in any context or situation you will encounter by applying our rules.

1. The **"a"** in Spanish is pronounced like the vowel sound in the English word "top."

Ana   La banana   radar   cantar

2. In Spanish, the **"e"** is similar to the "e" in the word "they."

le   Elena   Pepe   tener me

3. The **"i"** in Spanish, and the word "y" are like the "i" in the word "Lisa."

vivir   sí   y   risco   María

4. In Spanish, the **"o"** is similar to the vowel sound in the English word "no."

rojo   motor   Toni   lote   ojo

5. The **"u"** in Spanish is like the vowel sound in the English word "root."

| duna | una | Lupe | Luna | gusto |

B. The different "R" sounds.

1. At the beginning of a word, the letter **"r"** is trilled or vibrated much like a cat purring. A double r (rr) in a word is also trilled.

| Ramón | corral | rosa | rana | parra |

2. In words when a single **"r"** appears before a consonant or **"a"** at the end of the word, the **"r"** is pronounced like a **"d."**

| pero | tarde | circo | leer |
| dormir | nadar | beber | cantar |

3. When a single **"r"** is between vowels or after a consonant, it is not trilled (vibrated) but rather pronounced like a **"d."**

| toro | pero | Mario | para |
| cara | Teresa | dinero | franco |

Repeat all of the words in this column:

1.	**au**	ow (now)	causa (COW-sah)
			auto (OW–toh)
2.	**ei**	ay (ray)	aceituna (ah-sey-TU-nah)
3.	**ai**	y (type)	fraile (FRY-lay)
4.	**ie**	yeh (yet)	cubierto (coo-BYEHR-toh)
5.	**ue**	weh (west)	bueno (BWEH-noh)
6.	**eu**	ay-oo	deuda (DAYOO-dah)
7.	**ia**	ee-ah (Korea)	diablo (dee-AH-blo)
8.	**io**	ee-o (Polio)	serio (sair-EE-OH)
9.	**iu**	ee-oo (see you)	ciudad (see-oo-DAH)
10.	**oi, oy**	oy (toy)	soy (so-HOY)
11.	**ua**	oo-ah (water)	agua (AH-gwa)
12.	**up**	woh (woe)	cuota (QWOH-tah)
13	**ui**	oo-ee (we)	cuidado (qwee-DAH-doo)
14.	**uy**	wee (we)	muy (MOO-wee)

CONSONANTS

Most Spanish consonants are pronounced the same as they are in English: b, d, f, k, l, m, n, p, q, s, t, w, x. The Spanish language contains three consonants which are not found in English: ch, ll, and ñ.

b	sounds like 'b' or 'v'	burro (BOO-ro)
c	(before a, o, u) hard k sound (cot)	campo (KAHM-po) cosa (KOH-sah)
c	(before e, i) soft s sound (cent)	centro (SEHN-troh) cinta (SEEN-tah)
cc	hard and soft cc (ks sound) (action)	acción (ahk-see-OHN)
ch	Hard ch sound (church)	muchacha (moo-CHAH.chah)
g	(before a, o, u) hard g (got)	gafas (GAH-fas) gozar (goh-ZAR)
g	(before e, i) breathy h (hat)	general (hen-eh-RAHL)
h	always silent	hotel (oh-TAIL)
j	breathy as in h sound (hat)	José (oh-SAY)

l	English l sound (lamp)	luna (LOO-nah)
ll	as in English y (yes)	rollo (RHO-yoh)
n	English n (no)	nadar (nah-DAR)
ñ	English ny (canyon)	señorita (seh-NYOH-ree-tah)
qu	English k (kite)	que (kay)
r	trilled only once	caro (KAH-roh)
rr	(or r at beginning of word, trilled strongly)	rico (RREE-koh) burro (BURR-oh)
s	English s (sit)	fosa (FOH-sah)
v	English b (book)	pavo (PAB-oh)
x	English s	extra (ES-trah)
y	English y (yes) (by itself y=i)	yo (yoh) y (ee)
z	English s	zumo (ZOO-moh)

ACCENT MARKS AND STRESS

1. Words ending in a vowel, **n**, or **s** are stressed on the next to the last syllable: para (PA-ra).

2. Words ending in any consonant, with the exception of **n** and **s**, are stressed on the last syllable: verdad (ver-DAD), vivir (vi-VIR) or motor (mo-TOR).

3. When a word does not follow the first two rules, a written accent has to be used: montón (mon-TON) or rápido (ra-PI-do).

PRONUNCIATION EXERCISE

NOTE: To get the most out the following pronunciation exercise, do not worry about the meaning of the words. You should concentrate on pronouncing the words correctly. Do not forget to stress the underlined syllables.

YUCA	MAYO	COCUYO	REY	FOTO	CAFÉ
TELÉFONO	YEMA	YATE	AYUDA	SOY	FARO
SOFÁ	BÚFALO	YOYO	RAYO	CABUYA	LEY
FILA	RIFA	FÁBULA			

JARA	JEFE	JINETE	OJO	HILO	HUMO
HOJA	JOYA	CAJA	ABEJA	AJO	HABA
HIJO	HACHA	JUGO	ROJO	CONEJO	AJÍ
HOJA	HOYO	HORA			

BAILE	ONIX	BOINA	HUEVO	TAXI	EXAMEN
EXCUSA	CIELO	PIANO	PEINE	INDIO	DEUDA

SEXO	MÁXIMO	SEXO	TORÁX	AULA	RUEDA
VIUDA	CUIDA	BOXEO	ÓXIDO	TEXTO	BÓRAX
TRUCO	SASTRE	PUPITRE	TRACTOR	BLUSA	MUELLE
CABLE	PÚBLICO	TREN	LITRO	LETRA	TRAPICHE
BLOQUE	PUEBLO	NIEBLA	AMABLE	TRIBU	POTRO
TRUCHA	ESTRELLA	SABLE	ESTABLO	HABLA	BLANCO
FRESA	FRENO	REFRESCO	PRIMO	CAPRICHO	PRIMERO
PROFESORA	FRITURA	FRASCO	FRAGUA	PRESO	PROMESA
PRINCESA	FRASE	FRUTERO	COFRE	PRADO	PREGUNTA
CIGÜEÑA	PINGÜINO	HIGÜERO	PADRE	CUADRO	PIEDRA
AGÜITA	AGÜERO	YEGÜITA	DROGA	MADRINA	VIDRIO
DRAMA	MADRE	LADRILLO	TRIPLE	MICROBIO	
PLACA	PLUMA	PLAYA	PLUTÓN	CRUDO	SECRETO
MICROBIO	PLUMA	COPLA	PLANCHA	PLOMO	CREDO
CRÁNEO	ESCRITURA	PLATA	TEMPLO	PLÁTANO	PLANETA
CRISTAL	CREMA	CRUCIFIJO			
MAMÁ	MIMA	AMO	PAPA	MAPA	PAPA
AMA	MAMÁ	MIMA	PIPA	PUMA	PIPA
MIMA	AMO	MAMÁ	PEPA	PIPA	PUMA
SAPO	MASA	PESA	OSO	TAPA	MATA
PITO	OSITO	SOPA	MES	PISO	ASA
TOMATE	PATO	META	MAMITA	SUMA	MISA
PESO	USO	TOSE	MOTO	PITA	PATITO
NENE	MANO	TINA	SEMANA	DADO	NIDO
MODA	LADO	NENA	PINO	MANÍ	PEPINO

DUDA	PIDE	NUDO	DAMA	NATA	TUNA
PENA	MINUTO	DEDO	SEDA	TODO	SODA
LUNA	SALA	LUPA	PILOTO	MURO	LIRA
TESORO	ARO	LIMA	PELO	LIMPIA	MALETA
PERA	MORA	MINERO	ERA	LOTE	TELA
MULA	PALOMA	TORO	DURO	MARINO	ORO
RISA	TORRE	RATA	PIÑA	LEÑA	PAÑO
AÑO	REMO	PERRO	ROSA	PUÑO	BAÑO
UÑA	SEÑA	ROPA	TARRO	RANA	MOÑO
NIÑO	DAÑO	RIÑA			
CAMA	COCO	PICO	ROCA	VASO	PAVO
AVE	VENA	COPA	CUÑA	BOCA	SACO
VELA	NAVE	VIDA	LAVA	CUNA	CASA
MICO	NUCA	VINO	UVA	VARA	VIVE

SPANISH TONGUE TWISTERS
TRABALENGUAS

Here are a few Spanish tongue twisters (*trabalenguas* in Spanish) that will help you improve your pronunciation. The English translation follows each tongue twister. Have fun!

Tres tristes tigres trigaban trigo en un trigal.
Three sad tigers were swallowing wheat in a wheat field.

¿Usted no nada nada? - No, no traje traje.
You don't swim at all? No, I didn't bring a (swim) suit.

Poquito a poquito Paquito empaca poquitas copitas en pocos paquetes.
Little by little Paquito is packing some wine glasses in a few boxes.

Un tubo tiró un tubo y otro tubo lo detuvo. Hay tubos que tienen tubos pero este tubo no tuvo tubo.
A pipe hit a pipe and another pipe stopped it. There are pipes that have pipes but this pipe had no pipe.

Juan junta juncos junto a la zanja.
Juan is gathering reeds by the ditch.

Mi caballo pisa paja, paja pisa mi caballo.
My horse steps on hay, hay is stepped on by my horse.

Jorge el cerrajero vende cerrajes en la cerrajería.
George the locksmith sells locks at the locksmith's shop.

Erre con "erre" cigarro, "erre" con "erre" barril.
Rápido corren los carros, Cargados de azucar del ferrocarril.
R with an "R," cigar. "R" with an "R," barrel. Rapid run the cars (of the train) loaded with the railroad's sugar.

El que poca papa gasta poca papa paga.
Who wastes few potatoes pays few potatoes.

El sapo sapote no come camote.
The sly frog eats no sweet potato.

Pablito clavó un clavito en la calva de un calvito.
En la calva de un calvito un clavito clavó Pablito.
Pablito nailed a nail in the bald patch of a small bald man

Como poco coco como, poco coco compro.
Because I eat little coconut, I buy little coconut.

Mi mamá me mima mucho.
My mother spoils me.

Pancha aplancha con cuatro planchas. ¿Con cuántas planchas aplancha Pancha?
Pancha irons with four irons. With how many irons does Pancha iron?

Pablito piso el piso, pisando el piso Pablito piso cuando Pablito piso el piso, piezas de piso piso Pablito.
Pablito stepped on the floor, while stepping on the floor Pablo stepped on the floor, pieces of the floor stepped on Pablo.

Corre pollo renco, corre calle arriba, correo pollo renco, corre por tu vida.
Run lame chicken, run upstreet, run lame chicken, run for your life.

Part II
Spanish Survival Phrases for Daily Situations

NOTE: Starting on the next page, the best way to use this book is to memorize one section at a time by repeating it as many times as necessary. Once you have mastered one section, go on to the following one.

Please see the note at the beginning of Part I about applying the simple pronunciation rules. By mastering them and the basic vowel sounds there is NO need for a standard phonetic pronunciation guide in this book. The idea is to eliminate students' need to be dependent on a pronunciation guide as a crutch and thus be able to pronounce words in any context or daily situation.

REPEAT ONLY IN SPANISH:

1. NAME / NOMBRE

What's your name?	*¿Cómo se llama usted?*
My name is	*Me llamo...*
It's a pleasure	*Mucho gusto.*
The pleasure is mine	*El gusto es mío.*

2. GREETINGS / LOS SALUDOS

Hello	*Hola/ Buenas.*
Excuse me! (attracting attention)	*¡Upe!*
Good morning	*Buenos días.*
May I introduce you to…	*Le presento a...*
How are you?	*¿Cómo le va?/ ¿Cómo está?*
Fine, thank you.	*Muy bien, gracias.*
And you?	*¿Y usted?*
So-so	*Regular.*
What's happening?	*¿Qué pasa?*
Nothing much	*Nada en particular.*
Good afternoon.	*Buenas tardes.*
Good night.	*Buenas noches.*
Good bye/See you later	*Adiós./ Hasta luego.*
It's a pleasure (to meet you	*Mucho gusto.*

3. ADDRESS / EL DOMICILIO

Where do you live?	*¿Dónde vive usted?*
I live…	*Yo vivo...*
I'm from	*Yo soy de...*
Where are you staying	*¿Dónde está usted hospedado?*

4. AGE / LA EDAD

How old are you?	*¿Cuántos años tiene usted?*
I'm…years old	*Yo tengo...años.*
Where were you born?	*¿Dónde nació usted?*
I was born in…	*Yo nací en...*

5. NUMBERS / LOS NÚMEROS

Cardinal Numbers

1	*Uno*	40	*Cuarenta*
2	*Dos*	50	*Cincuenta*
3	*Tres*	60	*Sesenta*
4	*Cuatro*	70	*Setenta*
5	*Cinco*	80	*Ochenta*
6	*Seis*	90	*Noventa*
7	*Siete*	100	*Cien*
8	*Ocho*	200	*Doscientos*
9	*Nueve*	300	*Trescientos*
10	*Diez*	400	*Cuatrocientos*
11	*Once*	500	*Quinientos*
12	*Doce*	600	*Seiscientos*
13	*Trece*	700	*Setecientos*
14	*Catorce*	800	*Ochocientos*
15	*Quince*	900	*Novecientos*
16	*Dieciséis*	1000	*Mil*
17	*Diecisiete*	2000	*Dos mil*
18	*Dieciocho*	1.000.000	*Un millón*
19	*Diecinueve*	2.000.000	*Dos millones*
20	*Veinte*		
21	*Veintiuno*		

Ordinal Numbers

22	*Veintidós*	First	*Primero (a)*
23	*Veintitrés*	Second	*Segundo (a)*
24	*Veinticuatro*	Third	*Tercero (a)*
25	*Veinticinco*	Fourth	*Cuarto (a)*
26	*Veintiséis*	Fifth	*Quinto (a)*
27	*Veintisiete*	Sixth	*Sexto (a)*
28	*Veintiocho*	Seventh	*Séptimo (a)*
29	*Veintinueve*	Eight	*Octavo (a)*
30	*Treinta*	Ninth	*Noveno (a)*
31	*Treinta y uno*	Tenth	*Décimo (a)*

6. DAYS OF THE WEEK / LOS DÍAS DE LA SEMANA - MONTHS / LOS MESES - SEASONS / ESTACIONES - DATE / LA FECHA

Days of the week

Monday	*Lunes*
Tuesday	*Martes*
Wednesday	*Miércoles*
Thursday	*Jueves*
Friday	*Viernes*
Saturday	*Sábado*
Sunday	*Domingo*

Seasons

Spring	*La primavera*
Summer	*El verano*
Fall	*El otoño*
Winter	*El invierno*

Months

January	*Enero*
February	*Febrero*
March	*Marzo*
April	*Abril*
May	*Mayo*
June	*Junio*
July	*Julio*
August	*Agosto*
September	*Septiembre*
October	*Octubre*
November	*Noviembre*
December	*Diciembre*

NOTE: In Costa Rica, there are only two seasons: the dry season (*estación seca / verano*) ranging from about December through April, and the rainy or wet season (*estación lluviosa / invierno*) ranging from about May through November.

Date

What day is today?	*¿Qué día es hoy?*
Today is	*Hoy es el...de...*
What month is it?	*¿Qué mes es?*
It's...	*Es...*
What's the date?	*¿Cuál es la fecha?*
It's...	*Es...*

7. COLORS / LOS COLORES

What color is it?	*¿De qué color es?*
What's your favorite color?	*¿Cuál es su color preferido?*
Black	*Negro*
Blue	*Azul*
Brown	*Café / Castaño*
Green	*Verde*

Orange	*Anaranjado*
Pink	*Rosado*
Purple	*Morado*
Red	*Rojo*
Yellow	*Amarillo*
White	*Blanco*

8. SHOPPING / IR DE COMPRAS

Bakery	*La panadería*
Book store	*La librería*
Barbershop	*La peluquería*
Beauty parlor	*El salón de belleza*
Butcher shop	*La carnicería*
Candy store	*La confitería*
Corner grocery store	*La pulpería* (CR)
Department store	*Tienda por departamentos*
Fish store	*La pescadería*
Flower shop	*La florería, floristería*
Greengrocer	*La verdulería*
Hardware store	*La ferretería*
Jewelry store	*La joyería*
Liquor Store	*La licorera*
Market	*El supermercado*
Newsstand	*Puesto de periódicos y revistas*
Pharmacy / drug store	*La farmacia*
Pastry Shop	*La pastelería*
Record store	*La tienda de discos*
Shoe store	*La zapatería*
Toy store	*La juguetería*
Souvenir store	*La tienda de recuerdos*
Sporting goods store	*La tienda de artículos deportivos*
Tailor	*La sastrería*

Open	*Abierto*
Closed	*Cerrado*

Cheap .... *Barato*
Expensive .... *Caro*
Sale .... *En oferta*
Small .... *Pequeño, small*
Medium .... *Mediano, médium*
Large .... *Grande, large*
Extra large .... *Extra grande, extra largo*

Can you wrap it? .... *¿Me lo puede envolver?*
Do you have another one? .... *¿Tiene otro parecido?*
Do you have others? .... *¿Tiene otros?*
Do you accept credit cards? .... *¿Aceptan tarjetas de crédito?*
Does it have a guarantee? .... *¿Tiene garantía?*
How much is it? .... *¿Cuánto es?/ ¿Cuánto vale?*
I want my money back .... *Favor de devolver mi dinero*
I'm just looking .... *Solo estoy viendo.*
I'll take it .... *Me lo llevo*
Put it in a bag .... *Póngamelo en una bolsa.*
There is something wrong with it .... *Es defectuoso.*
What color does it come in? .... *¿Qué colores tiene?*
What size? .... *¿Qué tamaño, talla?*
Wrap it .... *Envuélvalo.*

9. SHOE STORE, SHORE REPAIR / ZAPATERIA

Arch .... *Empeine*
Arch supports .... *Plantillas*
Boot .... *Bota*
Closed shoe .... *Zapato cerrado*
Corns .... *Callos*
Heel (of foot) .... *Talón*
Heel (of shoe) .... *Tacón*
Loafer .... *Mocasines*
Low-cut boot .... *Botín*
Open shoe .... *Zapato abierto*

Polish	*Dar lustre/ sacarle brillo*
Put soles on the shoes	*Póngale suelas a los zapatos*
Sandle	*Sandalia/ chancleta*
Sew shoe	*Coser el zapato*
Shoe horn	*Calzador*
Shoe laces	*Cintas/ cordones*
Shoemaker	*Zapatero*
Shoe tree	*Horma*
Slipper	*Pantufla*
Sole	*Suela*
Stretch (a shoe)	*Estirar*
Taps	*Tapillas*
Tip	*Punta*
Toe	*El dedo del pie*
Tongue of shoe	*Lengüeta*
Too long	*Me quedan largos*
Too short	*Me quedan cortos*
Too tight	*Me aprietan*
Uncomfortable (plural)	*Incómodos*
Upper part of shoe	*Pala*
What Length?	*¿Qué largo?*
What size?	*¿Qué número?*
What width?	*¿Qué ancho?*
Widen a shoe	*Ensanchar*

Bargaining

Very expensive	*Muy caro*
Cheaper	*Más barato*
Can you lower the price?	*¿Puede bajar el precio?*
I'll give you 20 colones	*Le doy 20 colones*
Last offer	*Ultima oferta*
I'm going	*Me voy*
I'll take it	*Me lo llevo*

10. LIKES/DISLIKES / GUSTOS

	Singular	Plural
I like	*Me gusta*	*Me gustan*
I don't like	*No me gusta*	*No me gustan*
You like	*Le gusta*	*Le gustan*
You don't like	*No le gusta*	*No le gustan*

11. SOCIAL SITUATIONS / SITUACIONES SOCIALES

What do you do?	*¿Qué hace usted?*
Do you have a boyfriend/girlfriend?	*¿Tiene novio/novia?*
What are your hobbies?	*¿Cuáles son sus pasatiempos?*
What's your phone number?	*¿Cuál es su número de teléfono?*
Would you like to go somewhere quieter?	*¿Le gustaría ir a un lugar más tranquilo?*
Would do you like to dance?	*¿Le gustaría bailar?*
You have beautiful eyes	*Tiene los ojos preciosos.*
You have a beautiful body	*Tiene buen cuerpo.*
You have a good personality	*Tiene una buena personalidad.*
Leave me alone!	*¡Déjame en paz!*
Do you want to go to the movies?	*¿Le gustaría ir al cine?*
Would you like to go out with me?	*¿Le gustaría salir conmigo?*
Would do you like to have lunch?	*¿Le gustaría almorzar?*
Would you like to have dinner with me?	*¿Le gustaría cenar conmigo?*
Are you free tomorrow?	*¿Está libre mañana?*
What plans do you have for..?	*¿Qué planes tiene para…?*
I'm busy	*Estoy ocupado/a.*
What about another day?	*¿Qué le parece otro día?*
What time shall we meet?	*¿A qué hora nos vemos?*
I'll meet you	*Nos encontramos.*
I'll pick you up at…	*Pasaré a las…*
My place or your place?	*¿Mi casa o tu casa?*
May I take you home?	*¿Me permite llevarla a su casa?*

What's your address?....................................¿Cuál es su dirección?

Can I come in for awhile?...........................¿Puedo entrar por un rato?

I like you..Me cae bien.

I love you...La (fem.) quiero/Lo (masc.) quiero.

You're attractive.......................................Eres muy atractiva/eres guapa.

Touch me here..Tócame aquí.

I like the way you kiss................................Me gusta como besas.

Would you like to make love?.....................¿Te gustaría hacer el amor
                                                                    conmigo?

Take off your clothes ....Quítate la ropa

I won't do it without protection..................No quiero hacerlo sin un preservativo.

Do you like that?......................................¿Te gusta?

Don't stop..No pares.

Faster..Más rápido.

Softer..Más suave.

It was great..¡Estuvo fantástico!

Did you have an orgasm?...........................¿Te viniste?

Can I stay all night?..................................¿Puedo quedarme?

We make a good couple ....Hacemos buena pareja.

I'll call you tomorrow ....Te llamaré mañana.

Will you write?...¿Me escribirá?

I don't like you ....No me simpatizas.

This isn't working.....................................Esto no funciona.

I'd like to stay friends...............................Me gustaría ser tu amigo.

12. NIGHTLIFE / LA VIDA NOCTURNA

Bar ....Bar

Bordel...Burdel

Casino ....Casino

Concert ....Concierto

Dancehall...Salón de baile

Discotheque ....La discoteca

Movies...*Cine*
Nightclub..*Centro nocturno*
Theater...*Teatro*
Is there a cover charge?..*¿Hay consumo mínimo?*
It's free...*Es gratis*
Is a reservation necessary?..................................*¿Hay que hacer una reservación?*
To party...*Andar de fiesta*
Party animal..*Fiestero*

13. DIRECTIONS / LAS INDICACIONES

Where is…?..*¿Dónde está...?*
Is this the road to…?...*¿Es este el camino a...?*
How do I get to?...*¿Cómo llego a...?*
                                                                               ¿Cuál es la mejor ruta hacia?
                                                                               ¿Por dónde voy mejor?
How far is it?..*¿A qué distancia queda?*
Can you repeat that, please?...............................*¿Puede repetírmelo, por favor?*
How long does it take by car?............................*¿Cuánto dura el viaje en carro?*
How long does it take on foot?..........................*¿Cuánto dura a pie?*

Far...*Lejos*
Near...*Cerca*
North...*Norte*
South...*Sur*
West...*Oeste*
East...*Este*
Straight ahead...*Derecho*
To the right..*A la derecha*
To the left...*A la izquierda*
In front of…...*Enfrente de…*
On the other side of the street...........................*Al otro lado de la calle*
Toward...*Hacia*
In the direction of…...*En la dirección a…*
This way...*Por aquí*

Go down (street)	*Baje*
Go up (street)	*Suba*
On the corner	*En la esquina*
Around the corner	*A la vuelta de la esquina*
Blocks	*Cuadras*
Traffic light	*Semáforo*
Wrong way	*Contra vía*
Intersection	*Cruce, intersección*
Meters	*Metros/varas (slang)*
Take the road to…	*Tome la carretera a…*
Follow the signs to…	*Siga las señales para…*
Follow me!	*¡Sígame!*
I'm lost	*Estoy perdido.*

14. STREET SIGNS / ROTULOS

Closed	*Cerrado*
Dangerous curve	*Curva peligrosa*
Detour	*Desviación/desvío*
Don't turn right	*No vire a la derecha*
Don't turn left	*No vire a la izquierda*
Drive carefully	*Maneje con cuidado*
End of pavement	*Fin del pavimento*
Exit	*Salida*
Intersection	*Cruce*
Keep right	*Conserva su derecha*
Lane closed	*Carril cerrado*
Loose gravel/sand	*Arena suelta*
Men working	*Hombres trabajando*
Merging traffic	*Caros entrando*
Narrow bridge	*Puente angosto*
Narrow road	*Camino angosto*
One lane	*Un solo carril*
One-way traffic	*Una vía*
Parking	*Parqueo*

Passing lane	*Carril de ascenso*
Road closed	*No hay paso*
Road under repair	*Tramo en reparación*
School	*Escuela*
Slippery surface	*Camino resbaloso*
Slow down	*Despacio*
Speed limit	*Velocidad máxima*
Stay to the right	*Conserve su derecha*
Stop!	*¡Alto!*
Toll booth	*Peaje*
Two-way traffic	*Doble vía*
Yield the right-of-way	*Ceda el paso*

15. EMERGENCY / LAS EMERGENCIAS

Accident	*Accidente*
Ambulance	*Ambulancia*
Crash	*Choque*
Danger	*Peligro*
Earthquake	*Terremoto*
Tremor	*Temblor*
Fire!	*¡Incendio!*
First aid	*Primeros auxilios*
Flood	*Inundación*
Help!	*¡Socorro! ¡Auxilio!*
Hurricane	*Huracán*
I had an accident	*Tuve un accidente.*
I lost my travelers checks	*Se perdieron mis cheques de viajero.*
I need help	*Necesito ayuda.*
I've been robbed	*Me robaron.*
I'm sick	*Estoy enfermo/a.*
I'm lost	*Estoy perdido/a.*
Is it safe?	*¿Es seguro?*
My...hurts	*Me duele...*
My bags got lost	*Se perdieron mis maletas.*
Pickpocket	*Carterista*
Paramedic	*Paramédico*
Rape	*Violación*

Robbery	Robo
Siren	Sirena
Smoke	Humo
Steal	Robar
Storm	Tormenta
Thief!	¡Ladrón!
Where is the bathroom?	¿Dónde está el baño?
Where is the hospital?	¿Dónde está el hospital?
Where is the pharmacy?	¿Dónde está la farmacia?
Where is the police station?	¿Dónde está la Comisaría?

16. POLICE / LA POLICIA

Bribe (not recommended)	Soborno / mordida
Car's papers (registration)	Los papeles del carro
Expired license	Licencia vencida
I haven't done anything bad	No he hecho nada malo.
I don't know the traffic rules here	No conozco las reglas viales de aquí.
I want to call a lawyer	Quiero llamar a un abogado.
I know my rights	Conozco mis derechos.
License	Licencia
Insurance	Seguros
No parking	Se prohibe estacionar
Parking meter	Parquímetro
Please let me go this time	Favor de dejarme ir esta vez
Please call me a tow truck	Favor de llamarme una grúa.
Police station	Comisaría, comandancia
Ticket	Parte (CR) / la multa
What have I done?	¿Qué he hecho?
Yearly registration	Marchamo
You are under arrest	Está detenido.
You are drunk	Está borracho / a.
You were speeding	Ha excedido la velocidad máxima.

17. GETTING A DRIVER'S LICENSE / LA OBTENCION DE UNA LICENCIA DE CONDUCTOR

Driver's license	*Licencia de conductor*
Driving test	*Examen práctico*
Driver's education	*Educación vial*
Expired	*Vencida*
Fill out the form	*Llene el formulario.*
Form	*Formulario*
Glasses	*Lentes*
Line for senior citizens	*Fila para gente mayor*
Line for handicapped	*Fila para discapacitados*
Medical examen	*Dictamen médico*
Number	*Número*
Photo	*Foto*
Renew	*Renovar*
Renewal	*Renovación*
Residency	*Residencia*
Stand in line	*Hacer fila*
Turn	*Turno*
Window	*Ventanilla*
Written exam	*Examen por escrito*
Valid	*Válida*

18. TELEPHONE / EL TELEFONO

Answering machine	*Contestadora*
Area code	*Código de área*
Calling card	*Tarjeta telefónica*
Can you speak more slowly?	*¿Podría hablar más despacio?*
Cell phone	*Celular*
Coin	*La moneda*
Collect	*Por cobrar*
Could you repeat that?	*¿Me lo repite, por favor?*
Credit card	*Tarjeta de crédito*
Extension	*Extención*

Hello	*Aló*
He/she is not home	*No se encuentra.*
I want to make a long distance call	*Quiero hacer una llamada de larga distancia.*
I want to make a local call	*Quiero hacer una llamada local.*
I'd like to speak to…	*Yo quisiera hablar con…*
Information	*Información*
I've been cut off	*Se cortó la llamada.*
Long distance	*Larga distancia*
Make a call	*Hacer una llamada.*
May I leave a message?	*¿Puedo dejar un recado?*
Message	*Mensaje/recado*
One moment, please	*Un momento, por favor*
Operator	*La operadora*
Pay here	*Pago aquí*
Pay phone	*Teléfono público*
Person to person	*Persona a persona*
Phone	*Teléfono*
Phone book	*La guía telefónica*
Phone booth	*Cabina telefónica*
Phone number	*Número de teléfono*
Please speak louder	*Favor de hablar más fuerte.*
Prepaid phone card	*Tarjeta telefónica*
Regular phone	*Teléfono fijo*
Reverse the charges/collect	*A cobrar allá/revertir los cargos*
Telephone bill	*Recibo de teléfono*
Telephone book	*Guía telefónica*
Telephone line	*Línea telefónica*
Telephone number	*Número telefónico*
The connection is bad	*No entra la señal.*
To dial	*Marcar*
What is the country code for…?	*¿Cuál es el código para…?*
When will he or she be back?	*¿A qué hora regresa?*
Where can I find a pay phone?	*¿Dónde queda el teléfono público?*

Whose calling?	*¿De parte de quién?*
Will you tell him or her I called?	*¿Podría decirle que llame?*
Would you ask him or her to call me?	*¿Podría decirle que me llame?*
Yellow pages	*Páginas amarillas*

19. INTERNET/EL INTERNET

Where is the closest internet cafe?	*¿Dónde queda el café internet más cercano?*
How much per hour?	*¿Cuánto cobra por hora?*
Do you have PCs?	*¿Tiene computadoras PC?*
Do you have Macs?	*¿Tiene Macintosh?*
I want to access my mail	*Me gustaría acceder mi correo.*
Can you help me?	*¿Me puede ayudar?*
I don't understand the Spanish keyboard	*No entiendo el teclado en español.*
How do I log on?	*¿Cómo me conecto?*
Can I use the printer?	*¿Puedo usar la impresora?*
Can I use the scanner?	*¿Puedo utilizar el escáner?*
Can I make a long distance call?	*¿Puedo hacer una llamada de larga distancia?*

20. BANKING AND MONEY EXCHANGE / LA BANCA Y CAMBIO DE DINERO

ATM	*Cajero automático*
Advance	*Adelanto*
Bank book	*Libreta*
Branch	*Sucursal*
Cash	*En efectivo*
Check	*Cheque*
Check book	*Chequera*
Checking account	*Cuenta corriente*
Credit card	*Tarjeta de crédito*
Debit card	*Tarjeta débito*

Deposit	*Depositar*
Drive-through teller	*Autobanco*
Identification	*La identificación*
Passport	*Pasaporte*
Safety deposit box	*Caja de seguridad*
Teller	*Cajero/a*
Travelers checks	*Cheques de viajero*
Window	*Ventanilla*
Withdraw money	*Retirar dinero*
I need change	*Necesito cambio*
I would like to change…	*Yo quisiera cambiar...*
Large bills	*Billetes grandes*
Small bills	*Billetes pequeños*

Can I exchange money here?	*¿Puedo cambiar dinero aquí?*
Can I have money transferred here from my home bank?	*¿Puedo mandar transferir plata de mi banco?*
Can I use my card in the ATM	*¿Puedo usar mi tarjeta en el cajero automático?*
Has my money arrived?	*¿Ha llegado mi dinero?*
How many colones per dollar?	*¿Cuántos colones por dólar?*
The ATM has eaten my card	*El cajero automático se ha tragado mi tarjeta.*
What time does the bank open?	*¿A qué hora abre el banco?*
What's the rate of exchange?	*¿A cómo está el cambio?*
What's your commission?	*¿Cuál es su comisión?*
Where are the ATMs?	*¿Dónde están los cajeros automáticos?*
Where can I exchange money?	*¿Dónde puedo cambiar dinero?*

21. CAR RENTAL / CARROS DE ALQUILER

Air conditioning	*Aire acondicionado*
Automatic	*Automático*

Big..*Grande*
Free mileage ....*Libre kilometraje*
Full insurance..*Cobertura total/seguro completo*
Insurance ....*Seguros*
Map..*Mapa*
Stick shift ....*De velocidades, marchas*

Can you show me how to get to…?.............*¿Puede indicarme el camino a…?*
Do you have an emergency
phone number?..*¿Tiene un número de emergencia?*
How much does it cost per week?...............*¿Cuánto cuesta por semana?*
How much per day?.......................................*¿Cuánto cuesta por día?*
I want to rent a car......................................*Quiero alquilar un coche*
Per kilometer?...*¿Por kilómetro?*
Small/compact ....*Pequeño/compacto*
What kind of fuel does it take?...................*¿Qué clase de gasolina usa?*
Where do I leave off the car ? ....*¿Dónde puedo dejar el carro?*

22. TAXI / EL TAXI

Available...*Libre*
Block..*Cuadra/cien metros/cien varas*
Diagonal to… ....*Diagonal a…*
East..*Este*
Intersection ....*Cruce/intersección*
Next to ....*Al lado de/a la par de/contiguo*
North ....*Norte*
South...*Sur*
Taxi meter...*La María/taxímetro*
Unavailable ....*Ocupado*
West...*Oeste*
Take me to… ....*Lléveme a…*
The address is… ....*La dirección es…*
The next street..*La próxima calle*
How much does it cost to...? ....*¿Cuánto me cobra a..?*

How much per hour?	¿Cuánto cobra por hora?
How much do I owe you?	¿Cuánto le debo?/¿Cuánto es?
Keep the change	Quédese con el vuelto
Stop at the corner!	¡Pare en la esquina!
Stop here!	¡Pare aquí!
Stop there!	¡Pare allí!
Taxi!	¡Taxi¡
Use the taxi's meter	Use la María, por favor
You are charging too much	Está abusando.
Wait	¡Espéreme!
Will you wait for me?	¿Me espera?

23. BUS / EL AUTOBUS

Are you going to…?	¿Va usted a…?
Bus stop	Parada de autobuses
Do I have to change buses?	¿Tengo que cambiar de autobús?
How far is…?	¿A qué distancia queda?
How often do the buses arrive /leave/pass by?	¿Con qué frecuencia llegan / salen/pasan los autobuses?
How much does it cost?	¿Cuanto cuesta el pasaje?
I'll get off here/ there	Me bajo aquí/allá
Is this the bus to…?	¿Es éste el autobus a…?
Stop!	¡Parada!
Stop here/there/at…	Pare aquí/allí/en la…
The next corner	Próxima esquina
The next stop	La próxima parada.
Where is the bus stop to...?	¿Dónde está parada de...?
Where is the bus terminal to…?	¿Dónde está la terminal de autobús de...?

24. HOTEL / EL HOTEL

Air conditioning	Aire acondicionado
Bath	Baño
Bellboy	Botones

Double room	*Habitación doble/ para dos personas*
Elevator	*Ascensor*
Ice	*Hielo*
I'm checking out	*Me marcho/ me voy*
Please send...to my room	*Haga el favor de mandar... a mi habitación.*
Queen/King size bed	*Cama matrimonial*
Single bed	*Cama individual*
Single room	*Habitación sencilla/ para una persona.*
Twin bed	*Camas gemelas*
Safety deposit box	*Caja de seguridad*
Shower	*Ducha*
Suitcase	*Maleta*
Towel	*Toalla*
Can you wake me up at... please	*Puede despertarme a la/ las... por favor.*

25. RESTAURANT / EL RESTAURANT

A piece of...	*Un pedazo de...*
Appetizer	*El aperitivo/ boca* (CR)
Artificial sweetener	*Endulzador artificial*
Baked	*Al horno/ horneado*
Barbecued	*Al carbón*
Bill	*La cuenta*
Bitter	*Amargo*
Boiled	*Hervido/ guisado*
Bread	*Pan*
Breaded	*Empanizado*
Breakfast	*El desayuno*
Broiled/grilled	*A la parrilla*
Butter	*Mantequilla*
Cooked over wood	*A leña*
Cup	*Taza*

Dinner	*La cena*
Doggie bag	*Una bolsa para el perro*
Dressing	*Aderezo*
Food's good/bad	*Está bueno/malo*
Fork	*Tenedor*
Fried	*Frito*
Fried eggs	*Huevos fritos*
Glass	*Vaso*
Grilled	*A la plancha/a la parrilla*
Fried	*Frito*
Hard bolied eggs	*Huevos duros*
Hot sauce	*Picante*
Ice	*Hielo*
In garlic	*Al ajillo*
Keep the change	*¡Quédese con el vuelto!*
Knife	*Cuchillo*
Lunch	*El almuerzo*
Main course	*El plato fuerte*
Mayonnaise	*Mayonesa*
Medium	*Término medio*
Menu	*El menú*
Mustard	*Mostaza*
Napkin	*Servilleta*
Oil	*Aceite*
Overdone	*Demasiado cocinado*
Pepper	*Pimienta*
Plate	*Plato*
Rare	*Poco cocido/rojo*
Roasted	*Asado*
Salad	*Ensalada*
Salt	*Sal*
Scrambled eggs	*Huevos revueltos*
Smoked	*Ahumado*
Soft boiled eggs	*Huevos pasados por agua*

Spoon	*Cuchara*
Steamed	*Al vapor*
Sugar	*Azúcar*
Teaspoon	*Cucharita*
Tip	*La propina*
To take out	*Para llevar*
To eat here	*Para comer acá*
Too tough	*Demasiado duro*
Underdone	*Poco cocinado*
Vegetarian	*Vegetariano*
Vinegar	*Vinagre*
Waiter	*Salonero/mesero*
Well done	*Bien cocido*
Wine list	*Lista de vinos*
A table for two, please	*Una mesa para dos, por favor*
Can I pay cash?	*¿Puedo pagar en efectivo?*
Can I pay by credit card?	*¿Puedo pagar con tarjeta de crédito?*
Can I have a receipt?	*¿Me podría dar un recibo/factura?*
Can you recommend some dishes?	*¿Puede recomendar algunos platos?*
For tonight	*Para esta noche*
For tomorrow	*Para mañana*
I would like…	*Yo quisiera…*
I'd like to resérve	*Yo quisiera hacer una reservación.*
In the non-smoking area	*En la sección de no fumadores*
Is the service included?	*¿Está incluido el servicio?*
It's all together	*Todo junto.*
Specialty of the house	*La especialidad de la casa.*
We are paying separately	*Pagamos por separado.*
We have a reservation	*Tenemos una reservación.*
What do you recommend	*¿Qué recomienda usted?*

26. BAR / BAR

A shot of…	*Un trago de…*
Snack	*Boca*
Beer	*Cerveza/birra*
Bottle	*Botella*
Brandy	*Coñac*
Champagne	*Champán*
Cheers!	*¡Salud!*
Costa Rican sugarcane drink	*Guaro*
Draft beer	*Cerveza cruda*
I'm drunk	*Estoy borracho*
Glass	*Vaso/copa* (for wine)
Light beer	*Cerveza liviana*
Mug	*Tarro/jarra*
Pitcher	*Pichel*
Red wine	*Vino tinto*
Rose	*Vino rosado*
Rum	*Ron*
Straight	*Solo*
Tequila	*Tequila*
Vodka	*Vodka*
Whisky	*Whisky*
White wine	*Vino blanco*
Wine	*Vino*

27. MOVIE / EL CINE - THEATER / EL TEATRO

Action movie	*Película de acción*
Acts	*Actos*
Admission/ticket(s)	*La entrada*
Are there seats available?	*¿Hay campo?*
Candy	*Confites*
Comedy	*Comedia*
Documentary	*Documental*
Does it have English subtitles?	*¿Tiene subtítulos en ingles?*
Drama	*Drama*
Horror movie	*Película de horror*

Is it in English?	¿Es en inglés?
Popcorn	Palomitas
Science fiction	Ciencia ficción
Show	La función/la tanda
What time does…begin/end?	¿A qué hora comienza/termina?

28. IMMIGRATION / MIGRACION

Application	Solicitud
Citizen	Ciudadano
Enter country	Entradas
Expired	Vencido
Extention	Prórroga
Fine	Multa
Form	Formulario
How long is it good?	¿Por cuánto tiempo es válido?
I want to renew…	Quiero renovar/extender...
Leave country	Salidas
Line	Fila
Passport/visa	El pasaporte/la visa
Photo	Foto
Residency	La residencia
Resident	Residente
Stamps	Timbres
Student	Estudiante
To deport	Deportar
To renew	Renew
Tourist card	La tarjeta de turismo
What window?	¿Qué ventanilla?
When does it run out?	¿Cuándo vence?
Work permit	Permiso de trabajo

29. CUSTOMS/LA ADUANA

Does anyone here speak English?	¿Hay alguién aquí que hable inglés?

Duty exemption	*Bonificado*
I have nothing to declare	*No tengo nada que declarar.*
I have a work permit	*Tengo un permiso de trabajo.*
I have a study permit	*Tengo un permiso de estudiante.*
I have residence	*Tengo residencia.*
I have…suitcase	*Tengo…maletas?*
I'm American	*Soy estadounidense.*
I'm Canadian	*Soy canadiense.*
I'm coming from…	*Vengo de…*
I'm here for…days, weeks, months	*Estoy aquí por…días, semanas, meses.*
I'm just passing through	*Estoy de paso.*
I'm on a tour	*Estoy en un tour.*
I'm on vacation	*Estoy de vacaciones.*
I'm travelling alone	*Viajo solo.*
I'm travelling with my family	*Viajo con mi familia.*
I'm with a group	*Estoy con un grupo.*
It's a gift	*Es un regalo.*
It's for my personal use	*Es de uso personal.*
Tax	*Impuesto*

30. CLOTHING / LA ROPA

Blouse	*La blusa*
Boots	*Las botas*
Cap	*Gorra*
Coat	*El abrigo*
Dress	*El vestido*
Hat	*El sombrero*
Jacket	*La chaqueta*
Large	*Grande*
Loose	*Flojo*
Long	*Largo*
Miniskirt	*La minifalda*
Pants	*El pantalón*
Pantyhose	*Las pantimedias*

Raincoat...*La capa*
Sandals..*Las sandalias/ chancletas*
Shoes...*Los zapatos*
Shirt..*La camisa*
Skirt..*La falda*
Short...*Corto*
Small...*Pequeño*
Socks...*Los calcetines/ medias* (CR)
Stockings..*Medias*
Suit..*El traje*
Sweater...*El suéter*
Swimsuit..*El traje de baño*
Tight...*Apretado*
Tie...*La corbata*
Underpants...*El calzoncillo*
Undershirt..*La camiseta*

31. UTENSILS / LOS CUBIERTOS
Fork...*El tenedor*
Glass..*El vaso*
Knife..*El cuchillo*
Napkin...*La servilleta*
Plate...*El plato*
Spoon...*La cuchara*
Teaspoon...*Cucharita*

32. FURNITURE, APPLIANCES AND HOUSEHOLD GOOD / LOS MUEBLES, ELECTRODOMESTICOS Y ENSERES
Air conditioner...*Aire acondicionado*
Arm chair..*Sillón*
Bed...*Cama*
Blanket...*Cobija*
Blender...*Batidora*
Bookcase..*Estante/ biblioteca*
Broom..*Escoba*

Carpet/rug	*Alfombra*
Chair	*Silla*
Chest of drawers	*Gavetero*
China	*Porcelana*
Coffee pot	*Cafetera*
Coffee table	*Mesa de centro*
Colander/strainer	*Coladera*
Curtain	*Cortina*
Desk	*Escritorio*
Dining room table	*Mesa de comedor*
Dishwasher	*Lavaplatos*
Dresser	*Tocador*
Dryer	*Secadora*
End table	*Mesa de noche*
Freezer	*Congelador*
Frying pan	*Sartén*
Funnel	*Embudo*
Furniture	*Mueble*
Grater	*Rayador*
Lamp	*Lámpara*
Household goods	*Enseres/menaje*
Microwave over	*Microondas*
Mirror	*Espejo*
Oven	*Horno*
Pillow	*Almohada*
Pillow case	*Funda*
Refrigerator	*Refrigeradora/refri*
Rug/carpet	*Alfombra*
Sheet (bed)	*Sábana*
Sofa	*Sofá*
Stove	*Estufa*
Table	*Mesa*
Television set	*Televisor/tele*
Toaster	*Tostador*

Tray	*Bandeja*
Vacuum cleaner	*Aspiradora*
Venetian blinds	*Persianas*
Wall paper	*Papel tapiz*
Washing machine	*Lavadora*

33. BARBER SHOP / LA PELUQUERÍA

Bald	*Calvo*
Beard	*La barba*
Close shave	*A ras*
Comb	*Peine*
Curls	*Colochos/rizos*
Cut short	*Rapar*
Cut a little off the top	*Corte un poquito de arriba.*
Cut a little off the back	*Corte un poquito de atrás.*
Cut a little off the sides	*Corte un poquite de los lados.*
Even up	*Emparejar*
Gray hair	*Canas*
Haircut	*Corte de pelo*
I need a haircut	*Quiero un corte de pelo.*
Long/short/trim	*Largo/corto/recorte*
A shave	*Una afeitada*
Make an appointment	*Sacar la cita*
Moustache	*El bigote*
Shampoo	*Champú*
Sideburns	*Las patillas*
Straight hair	*Pelo lacio*
To brush	*Cepillar*
To comb	*Peinar*
To part hair	*Hacerse la raya/carrera*
To shave	*Afeitar or rasurar*
Wavy hair	*Pelo ondulado*

34. BEAUTY PARLOR / EL SALON DE BELLEZA

Back...*Atrás*
Curlers..*Rulos*
Cut in layers..*Cortar en capas*
Dark (color)..*Oscuro*
Don't cut it too short..................................*No lo quiero demasiado corto.*
Dry it for me..*Séquemelo*
Dye..*Tinte*
Front...*Enfrente*
Highlighted...*Rayos*
I'd like to make an appointment...............*Yo quisiera sacar una cita.*
Light (color)...*Claro*
Manicure...*Manicure/ manicura*
Nails...*Las uñas*
On top..*Arriba*
Paint nails..*Pintarse las uñas*
Pedicure...*Pedicure/ pedicura*
Permanent..*Una permanente*
Shampoo...*Lavar/ hacer el champú*
Sides...*Los lados*
Straighten hair...*Alisar*
Thin out..*Entresacar*

35. MARKET / EL MERCADO

Aisle..*Pasillo*
Can..*Lata*
Cash register...*La caja*
Cereal..*Cereal*
Cheese...*Queso*
Express..*La caja rápida*
Fish..*Pescado*
Fruit...*La fruta*
Meat...*La carne*
Vegetables...*Las verduras*

Where's...? .... *¿Dónde está...?*

36. AIRLINES / LINEAS AEREAS
Airplane .... *Avión*
Arrival .... *Llegada*
Aisle .... *Pasillo*
Are there flights to...? .... *¿Hay vuelos a...?*
Departure .... *Salida*
First class .... *Primera clase*
Gate .... *La Puerta*
One way .... *Boleto de ida*
Round trip ticket .... *Boleto de ida y vuelta*
Return .... *Boleto de regreso*
Seat .... *Asiento*
Smoking .... *Sección de fumar*
Ticket .... *Tiquete / boleto*

37. TRAVEL AGENCY / AGENCIA DE VIAJES
At what time does...leave/arrive? .... *¿A qué hora llega / sale...?*
First/second class .... *Primera / segunda clase*
How much is a ticket to...? .... *¿Cuánto vale un boleto a...?*
I am going to travel to... .... *Voy a viajar a...*

38. TRAIN STATION / ESTACIÓN DE TREN
A ticket to .... *Un boleto para...*
At what time does...leave/arrive? .... *¿A qué hora sale / llega...?*
Schedule .... *El horario*
Where does it leave from? .... *¿De dónde sale?*

39. GAS STATION / LA GASOLINERA
CAR TROUBLE/AVERIA
Air .... *Aire*
Battery .... *La batería*
Brake .... *Freno*

Bumper	*Parachoques*
Car body	*Carrocería*
Clutch	*El clutch (embrague)*
Body shop	*Enderezado y pintura*
Breaks	*Los frenos*
Brake shoes	*Zapatas*
Brake linings	*Pastillas*
Breakdown	*Avería*
Can you fix my tire?	*¿Puede arreglar mi llanta?*
Check the oil/water/battery/tires	*Revise el aceite/ el agua/ la batería/ las llantas.*
Dashboard	*Tablero de instrumentos*
Engine	*El motor*
Fan	*El ventilador*
Fan belt	*Faja de ventilador*
Fill it	*Llene el tanque*
Give me 10,000 colones worth of gasoline	*Deme 10,000 colones (pesos, etc.) de gasolina*
Filter	*Filtro*
I have a flat tire	*Mi llanta está desinflada/ pinchada.*
Gas tank	*Tanque*
Gas station	*Bomba (CR), Estación de servicio*
Generator	*Generador*
Headlight	*Faro/ luz delantera*
Hood	*Capota/ tapa*
Horn	*Bocina/ pito*
I need a push	*Necesito un empujón.*
I'm stuck	*Estoy varado.*
I need a tow	*Necesito una grúa.*
Is there a gas station near here?	*¿Hay una bomba por aquí?*
Jack	*Gata*
License plate	*Placa*
Lights	*Luces*
My car's broken	*Mi coche no funciona / está descompuesto.*

Makes a strange noise	*Hace un ruido extraño.*
Mechanic	*Mecánico*
Mechanic's shop	*Taller*
Mirror	*Espejo*
Motor / engine	*Motor*
Muffler	*Mufla*
My car overheats	*Mi carro sobrecalienta.*
My car is out of gas	*Me quedé sin gasolina.*
Please adjust the clutch	*Favor de ajustar el clutch.*
Please bleed the brakes	*Favor de purgar los frenos.*
Radiator	*El radiador*
Something smells like it is burning	*Huele a quemado.*
Spark plugs	*Las bujías/ candelas* (CR)
Spare tire	*La llanta de repuesto, refacción.*
The keys are locked inside the car	*La llaves están encerradas adentro del carro.*
The motor makes a strange noise	*El motor hace un sonido raro.*
The battery is dead	*La batería está muerta/ descargada.*
The steering doesn't work	*La dirección está descompuesta.*
The radiator has a leak	*El radiador tiene un hueco.*
There is a short circuit	*Hay un cortocircuito.*
Transmissión	*Transmisión*
Trunk	*Baúl/ cajuela*
Tune the motor	*Favor de afinar el motor.*
Turn signal	*Direccional*
Wash the car	*Favor de lavar el carro.*
Windshield	*Parabrisas*
Windshield wiper	*El limpiaparabrisas*
Won't start	*No arranca.*

40. FOOD / LA COMIDA

Fish	*Pescado*
Anchovies	*Anchoas*
Bass	*Corvina*
Clams	*Almejas*
Cod	*Bacalao*

Crab	*Cangrejo*
Crawfish	*Langostino*
Eel	*Anguila*
Herring	*Arenque*
Lobster	*Langosta*
Mussels	*Mejillones*
Octopus	*Pulpo*
Oyster	*Ostra*
Raw fish dish	*Ceviche*
Red snapper	*Pargo*
Salmon	*Salmón*
Sardine	*Sardina*
Shrimp	*Camarones*
Squid	*Calamares*
Trout	*Trucha*
Tuna	*Atún*
Poultry	*Aves*
Chicken	*Pollo*
Duck	*Pato*
Turkey	*Pavo*
Meat	*Carne*
Bacon	*Tocineta*
Chops	*Chuletas*
Ham	*Jamón*
Kidney	*Riñon*
Lamb	*Cordero*
Liver	*Hígado*
Loin (meat)	*Lomo*
Pork	*Carne de cerdo / puerco*
Pork sausage	*Chorizo*
Sausage	*Salchicha*

Steak	*Bistec*
Tongue	*Lengua*
Veal	*Ternera*
Vegetables	*Vegetales*
Artichoke	*Alcachofa*
Asparagus	*Espárragos*
Avocado	*Aguacate*
Beans	*Frijoles*
Beet	*Remolacha*
Bell pepper	*Pimiento/chile dulce* (CR)
Broccolli	*Brócoli*
Cabbage	*Repollo*
Carrots	*Zanahorias*
Cauliflower	*Coliflor*
Celery	*Apio*
Corn	*Maíz*
Corn on the cob	*Elote*
Cucumber	*Pepino*
Eggplant	*Berenjena*
Lentil	*Lenteja*
Lettuce	*Lechuga*
Lima bean	*Haba*
Mushroom	*Hongo/champiñón*
Olives	*Aceitunas*
Onion	*Cebolla*
Peas	*Guisantes*
Potato	*Papa*
Pumpkin	*Calabaza*
Radish	*Rábano*
Spinach	*Espinaca*
Squash	*Calabaza*
String beans	*Vainicas*

Sweet potato	*Camote*
Tomato	*Tomate*

Fruit	*Frutas*
Apple	*Manzana*
Apricot	*Albaricoque*
Banana	*Banano*
Blackberry	*Mora*
Cherry	*Cereza*
Date	*Dátil*
Fig	*Higo*
Grapefruit	*Toronja*
Grapes	*Uvas*
Lemon	*Limón*
Mango	*Mango*
Mandarin orange/tangerine	*Mandarina*
Melon	*Melón*
Orange	*Naranja*
Palm fruit	*Pejibaye* (CR)
Papaya	*Papaya*
Peach	*Durazno/melocotón*
Pear	*Pera*
Pineapple	*Piña*
Plantain	*Plátano*
Plumb	*Ciruela*
Raisin	*Pasa*
Rasberry	*Frambuesa*
Strawberry	*Fresas*
Watermelon	*Sandía*

Spices	*Especias*
Basil	*Albahaca*
Capers	*Alcaparra*
Cinnamon	*Canela*

Garlic	*Ajo*
Herb	*Hierba*
Horse radish	*Rábano picante*
Ketchup	*Salsa de tomate*
Mayonnaise	*Mayonesa*
Mint	*Hierba buena/menta*
Mustard	*Mostaza*
Parsely	*Perejil*
Pepper	*Pimienta*
Rosemary	*Romero*
Saffron	*Azafrán*
Salt	*Sal*
Sugar	*Azúcar*
Vinegar	*Vinagre*

Dessert	*Postre*
Cake	*Pastel/queque*
Candy	*Confites/dulces*
Candy bar	*Barra de chocolate*
Cookie	*Galleta*
Custard	*Flan*
Ice cream	*Helados*
Rice and Milk	*Arroz con leche*
Cream cake (with three kinds of milk)	*Tres leches* (CR)

Beverages	*Bebidas*
Beer	*Cerveza*
Coffee	*Café*
Cold	*Frío*
Hot	*Caliente*
Juice	*Jugo*
Milk	*Leche*
Mineral water	*Agua mineral*
Rice-based drink (orgeat)	*Horchata*

Soft drink	*Gaseosa*
Tea	*Té*
Wine	*Vino*
Pancakes	*Panqueques*
Corn Pancakes	*Chorreada* (CR)
Eggs	*Huevos*
Hazelnut	*Avellana*
Honey	*Miel*
Noodles	*Fideos*
Peanut	*Maní*
"Spotted rooster" (rice and beans)	*Gallo Pinto* (Costa Rican dish)
Rolls	*Arrolladitos*
Rice	*Arroz*
Spaghetti	*Macarrones*
Wheat	*Trigo*
Whole wheat	*Trigo integral*

41. POST OFFICE / EL CORREO

A stamp for	*Una estampilla para…*
Abroad	*Al extranjero*
Address	*Dirección*
Addresse	*Detinatario*
Air mail	*Correo aéreo*
Delivery	*Entrega*
Envelope	*Sobre*
Express, special delivery	*Entrega inmediata*
General delivery	*Lista de correo*
How long will it take to…?	*¿Cuánto tardará en llegar a…?*
I would like to send a letter to…	*Yo quisiera mandar una carta a…*
Is there any mail for me?	*¿Hay una carta para mí?*
It contains	*Contiene*
Letter	*La carta*
Letter carrier	*Cartero*
Mail box	*Buzón*

Mail delivery	*Entrega*
Mexico/U.S./Canada	*México/E.E.U.U./Canadá*
Package	*Paquete*
Pick up	*Recolección*
P.O. Box (address)	*Apartado*
P.O. Box (slot)	*Casilla*
Postcard	*La tarjeta postal*
Postman	*Cartero*
Registered mail	*Certificado*
Regular mail	*Correo regular*
Return address	*Dirección del remitente*
Special delivery	*Entrega inmediata*
Stamp	*Estampilla*
To insure	*Asegurar*
To send	*Enviar*
What's the postage for?	*¿Cuál es el porte para…?*
Where is the mailbox?	*¿Dónde está el buzón?*
Where is the nearest post office?	*¿Dónde queda el correo más cercano?*
Window	*Ventanilla*

42. LAUNDRY / LAVANDERÍA

Bleach	*El blanqueador*
Clean	*Limpiar*
Dirty	*Sucio/a*
Dry cleaners	*La tintorería*
Dry clean	*Lavar en seco*
Iron (verb)	*Planchar/aplanchar* (CR)
Ironing	*Planchado*
Laundromat	*Lavandería automática*
Lining (of a coat)	*Forro*
Mend	*Remendar*
Sleeve	*Manga*

Soap	*El jabón (detergente)*
Starch	*Almidón*
Starched	*Almidonado*

43. LOTTERY / LOTERIA

A type of lottery sold during the week	*Chance*
A single lottery ticket	*Pedazo*
Christmas lottery	*El gordo navideño*
In what newspaper can I get the lottery results?	*¿En qué periódico salen los resultados?*
Grand prize	*El premio gordo or premio mayor*
Lottery	*Lotería*
Lucky number	*Número de suerte*
The whole sheet of tickets	*Entero*
Type of scratcher or instant lotery	*Raspa*
Where can I claim my prize?	*¿Dónde puedo reclamar mi premio?*
Win the lottery	*Pegar/ganar la lotería*

44. THE BODY / EL CUERPO

Ankle	*Tobillo*
Appendix	*Apéndice*
Arm	*Brazo*
Back	*Espalda*
Bladder	*Vejiga*
Bone	*Hueso*
Chest	*Pecho*
Ear	*Oreja*
Eye	*Ojo*
Face	*Cara*
Finger	*Dedo*
Foot	*Pie*
Gland	*Glándula*

Hand	*Mano*
Hair	*Pelo*
Head	*Cabeza*
Heart	*Corazón*
Hip	*Cadera*
Jaw	*La mandíbula*
Joint	*Coyuntura/articulación*
Kidney	*Riñón*
Knee	*Rodilla*
Knuckle	*Nudillo*
Leg	*Pierna*
Lip	*Labio*
Little finger	*Dedo meñique*
Lung	*Pulmón*
Middle Finger	*Dedo medio*
Mouth	*Boca*
Muscles	*Músculos*
Neck	*Cuello*
Nose	*Nariz*
Penis	*Pene*
Ring finger	*Dedo anular*
Shoulder	*Hombro*
Stomach	*Estómago*
Teeth	*Dientes*
Thigh	*Muslo*
Throat	*Garganta*
Thumb	*Pulgar/dedo gordo*
Toe	*Dedo del pie*
Tongue	*Lengua*
Tonsils	*Amígdalas*
Vagina	*Vagina*
Waist	*Cintura*
Wrist	*Muñeca*

Bodily Sensations

To be cold...*Tener frío*
To be hot ....*Tener calor*
To be hungry...*Tener hambre*
To be sleepy ....*Tener sueño*
To be thirsty...*Tener sed*

45. MEDICAL / MEDICO

A cold...*Un resfriado*
Acne..*Acné*
Apendicitis...*Apendicitis*
Arthritis...*Artritis*
Asthma...*Asma*
Bleeding...*Sangrado*
Bone...*Hueso*
Bruise..*Un moretón*
Burn...*Quemaduras*
Cardiologist...*Cardiólogo*
Chills..*Escalofríos*
Chicken pox ....*Varicela*
Choke...*Atragantarse*
Contact lenses...*Lentes de contacto*
Cough...*Tos*
Cramps...*Calambres*
Crutches...*Muletas*
Cut...*Cortadura*
Dermatologist...*Dermatólogo*
Diarrhea...*Diarrea*
Diabetic...*Diabético*
Diet..*Dieta*
Dizzy..*Mareos*
Doctor..*El médico / doctor*
Dose...*Dosis*
Emergency room..*La sala de urgencias*

Epilepsy .... *Epilepsia*

Epileptic .... *Epiléptico*

Fever .... *Fiebre*

Flu .... *Gripe*

Gastroenterologist .... *Gastroenterólogo*

Gynecologist .... *Ginecólogo*

Food poisoning .... *Intoxicación*

Handicapped .... *Incapacitado / minusválido*

Headache .... *Dolor de cabeza*

High blood presssure .... *Presión alta*

I have… .... *Tengo...*

I'm allergic to… .... *Soy alérgico a…*

Indigestión .... *Indigestión*

Internist .... *Internista*

Itch .... *Picazón*

Laryrigitis .... *Laringitis*

Mumps .... *Paperas*

My…hurts .... *Me duele el (la)…*

Neurologist .... *Neurólogo*

Nose ears and throat doctor .... *Otorrinolaringólogo*

Ophthalmologist .... *Oftalmólogo*

Orthopedic surgeon .... *Ortopédico*

Pacemaker .... *Marcapasos*

Pediatrician .... *Pediatra*

Pneumonia .... *Pulmonía / neumonía*

Poisoning .... *Envenenamiento*

Period .... *Regla*

Rash .... *Salpullido / ronchas*

Sciatic .... *Ciática*

Sore throat .... *Dolor de garganta*

Sneeze .... *Estornudo*

Sprain .... *Torcedura*

Spasm .... *Espasmo*

Specialist .... *Especialista*

Stomach ache	*Dolor de estómago*
Sunburn	*Quemadura del sol*
Suppository	*Supositorio*
Surgeon	*Cirujano*
Swollen	*Hinchado*
Temperature	*Temperatura*
Tonsilitis	*Amigdalitis*
Ulcer	*Ulcera*
Unconscious	*Inconsciente*
Urologist	*Urólogo*
I feel…	*Me siento…*
Sick	*Enfermo/a*
Depressed	*Deprimido/a*
Strange	*Raro/a*
Better	*Mejor*
The same	*Igual*
Worse	*Peor*
Weak	*Débil*

46. DENTIST / DENTIST

Abscess	*Flemón/absceso*
Anesthetic	*Anestésico*
Braces	*Frenillo*
Bridge	*Puente*
Crown	*Corona*
Dentist	*El dentista*
False tooth	*Diente postizo*
Filling	*Empaste*
Floss	*Hilo dental*
Gums	*Encías*
I have a toothache	*Me duele una muela*
I have a cavity	*Tengo un diente picado/caries*
Molar	*Muela*
My gum hurts	*Me duele la encía*

Orthodontist	*Ortodoncista*
Rinse	*Enjuagar*
Tooth	*Diente*
Toothache	*Dolor de muela*
Toothbrush	*Cepillo de dientes*
X-ray	*Radiografía*

47. PHARMACY / LA FARMACIA

Antibiotic	*Antibiótico*
Aspirin	*Aspirina*
At night	*Por la noche*
Bandage	*Venda*
Bandaid	*Vendita*
Bobbypins	*Prensas*
Birth control pill	*Anticonceptivo*
Can you fill this prescription for me?	*¿Puede prepararme esta receta?*
Cold	*El resfriado*
Cologne	*Colonia*
Cough	*La tos*
Decongestant	*Descongestionate*
Dye	*Tinte*
How many times per day?	*¿Cuántas veces por día?*
In the morning	*Por la mañana*
I'm sick	*Estoy enfermo*
Indigestion	*Indigestión*
Is it suitable for children?	*¿Es apropiado para niños?*
Laxative	*Laxante*
Lipstick	*Lápiz labial*
Headache	*Dolor de cabeza*
Heartburn	*Acidez*
Makeup	*Maquillaje*
Mouth wash	*Enjuague bucal*
Nausea	*Náuseas*
Nail polish	*Esmalte para las uñas*

Ointment	*Ungüento*
Perfume	*Perfume*
Pharmacist	*El boticario / farmacéutico*
Pill	*La pastilla*
Prescription	*La receta*
Razor blade	*Hoja de afeitar*
Shampoo	*Champú*
Shaving cream	*Crema de afeitar*
Shot	*Inyección*
Sleeping pill	*Pastilla para dormir*
Soap	*Jabón*
Talcum powder	*Talco*
Tampons	*Tampones*
Toothache	*Dolor de muela*
What do you have for…?	*¿Qué tiene para...?*
Will it make me sleepy?	*¿Me dará sueño?*

48. VETERNARY / VETERINARIA

Animal hospital	*Clínica veterinaria*
Bird	*Pájaro*
Baby dog	*Cachorro*
Boarding	*Hospedaje*
Cat	*Gato / a*
Cat food	*Comida para gato*
Deworm	*Desparasitar*
Dog food	*Comida para perro*
Distemper	*Moquillo*
Dog	*Perro / a*
Fleas	*Pulgas*
Foot (of an animal)	*Pata*
Mange	*Sarna*
Litter	*Camada*
Neuter (male)	*Castrar*
Neuter (female)	*Sacar los ovarios*

Pet .... *Mascota*
Rabies .... *Rabia*
Ticks .... *Garrapatas*
Vet .... *Veterinario/a*
Shot .... *Vacuna/inyección*
Sick .... *Enfermo/a*
Wings .... *Alas*

49. COMPUTER LANGUAGE / LENGUAJE COMPUTACIONAL

Accessories .... *Accesorios*
Attached files .... *Archivos adjuntos*
Backup copy .... *Copia de respaldo*
Bookmark .... *Marcador*
Boot .... *Arrancar*
Browse .... *Navegar*
Cable .... *Cable*
Cartridge .... *Cartucho*
CD burner .... *Quemador de CD*
Command .... *Comando*
Compatible .... *Compatible*
Compress files .... *Comprimir archivos*
Computer .... *Computadora*
Computer crash .... *Se cayó el sistema*
Connect .... *Conectar*
Cursor .... *Cursor*
Data .... *Datos*
Data processing .... *Informatica*
Decompress files .... *Decomprimir archivos*
Download .... *Descargar*
Drag .... *Arrastrar*
E-mail .... *El correo electrónico*
File .... *Archivo*
Firewall .... *Muro de protección*
Floppy disk .... *Disco flexible*

Go back	*Regresar*
Go forward	*Adelantar*
Hacker	*Pirata*
Hard drive	*Disco duro*
Home page	*Página principal*
Hosting	*Hospedaje*
Icon	*Icono*
Ink	*Tinta*
Ink-jet printer	*Impresora de inyección*
Install	*Instalar*
Internal drive	*Disco interno*
Keyboard	*El teclado*
Laptop computer	*Computadora portátil*
Laser printer	*Impresora láser*
Memoria	*Memoria*
Menu	*Menu*
Modem	*Módem*
Monitor	*Monitor*
Mouse	*Ratón*
Network	*Red*
Networking	*Conexión de redes*
Operating system	*Sistema operativo*
Password	*Contraseña*
PC	*Computadora personal*
Port	*Puerto*
Printer	*Impresora*
On line	*En línea*
Upload	*Subir o cargar*
Save	*Guardar*
Screen	*La pantalla*
Search engine	*Buscador*
Secure web site	*Sitio web seguro*
Server	*Servidor*
Spam	*Correo basura/ no deseado*

Surf.. *Navegar*
To scan... *Escanear*
To hack .... *Piratear*
Tool Bar .... *Barra de herramientas*
Unsubscribe .... *Borrarse de una lista de suscriptores*
User friendly................................. *Fácil de usar*
User name .... *Nombre de usuario*
Upgrade .... *Actualizar*
URL.. *La dirección del sitio*
User name .... *Nombre de usuario*
Virus... *Virus*
Web... *La red*
Web camera.................................... *Cámara web*
Web design .... *Diseño de los sitio web*
Web site.. *Un sitio web*
Wirelesss .... *Inalámbrico*

50. MEASUREMENTS / CANTIDADES Y MEDIDAS

A couple of…................................. *Un par de...*
A little….. *Un poquito de...*
A lot.. *Mucho*
Enough .... *Bastante/ suficiente*
Half .... *La mitad*
Kilogram... *Un kilogramo*
Pound.. *Una libra*
Too much .... *Demasiado*

51. INSTRUCTIONS FOR DOMESTIC WORKERS / INSTRUCCIONES PARA EMPLEADAS DOMESTICAS

Bring me…....................................... *Tráigame...*
Can you recommend a reliable
babysitter?...................................... *¿Me puede recomendar una niñera confiable?*

Broom	*Escoba*
Change…	*Cambie…*
Clean…	*Limpie…*
Dust…(verb)	*Quítele el polvo a…*
Fold…	*Doble…*
How long did you work there?	*¿Por cuánto tiempo trabajó allí?*
Iron…	*Plumb…*
Letter of recommendation	*Carta de recomendación*
Mop	*Palo de piso*
Please…	*Por favor…*
Polish…	*Sáquele brillo a…*
Prepare…	*Prepare…*
Put away	*Guarde…*
References	*Referencias*
Straighten…	*Arregle/ acomode…*
Sweep…	*Barra…*
Take…	*Lleve…*
Take out…	*Saque…*
Take out the trash	*Saque la basura por favor.*
Vacuum…	*Pásele la aspiradora a…*
Vacuum cleaner	*Aspiradora*
Wash…	*Lave…*
Watch…	*Cuide…*
Watch the children	*Cuide los niños*
Water…	*Riegue/ póngale agua a…*
Wax…	*Encere…*

52. FINDING WORK / BUSCANDO TRABAJO

Application	*Solicitud*
Date of birth	*Fecha de nacimiento*
Education	*Estudios realizados*
Full-time	*Tiempo completo*
How much does the job pay?	*¿Cuánto pagan?*
I'm looking for work	*Ando buscando trabajo*
I'm experienced	*Tengo experiencia*

I'm bilingual .... *Soy bilingüe*
Letter of recommendation .... *Carta de recomendación*
Name .... *Nombre*
Nationality .... *Nacionalidad*
Part time .... *Tiempo parcial*
Place of birth .... *Lugar de nacimiento*
Resume .... *Currículum*
Steady work .... *Trabajo fijo*
What are the working hours? .... *¿Cuáles son las horas de trabajo?*
Work permit .... *Permiso de trabajo*

53. WEATHER / EL TIEMPO

Drizzle .... *Llovizna/*
Pelo de gato (CR)
It's cold .... *Hace frío*
It's drizzling .... *Está lloviznando*
It's hot .... *Hace calor*
It's cloudy .... *Está nublado*
It's cool .... *Hace fresco*
It's lightning .... *Relampagea*
It's muggy/humid .... *Está húmedo/está bochornoso*
It's sunny .... *Hace sol*
It's thundering .... *Truena*
It's windy .... *Hace viento*
It's raining .... *Llueve*
It's foggy .... *Hay neblina*
Lightning bolt .... *Rayo*
Storm .... *Tormenta*
The weather is good .... *Hace buen tiempo*
The weather is bad .... *Hace mal tiempo*
Thunder .... *Trueno*
Tornado .... *Tornado*
What's the weather like? .... *¿Qué tiempo hace?*
Wind .... *Viento*

54. PEOPLE / GENTE

Aunt...*Tía*
Brother..*Hermano*
Brother-in-law..*Cuñado*
Boyfriend...*Novio*
Cousin...*Primo/a*
Daughter..*Hija*
Daughter-in-law...*Nuera*
Father...*Padre*
Father-in-law..*Suegro*
Girlfriend...*Novia*
Grandchild...*Nieto/a*
Grandfather..*Abuelo*
Grandmother...*Abuela*
Great grandfather..*Bisabuelo*
Great grandmother...*Bisabuela*
Husband...*Marido*
Mother..*Mamá/madre*
Nephew...*Sobrino*
Parents..*Padres*
Relatives..*Parientes*
Sister...*Hermana*
Sister-in-law..*Cuñada*
Son..*Hijo*
Son-in-law...*Yerno*

55. FINDING AN APARTMENT OR HOUSE / ENCONTRAR UN APARTAMENTO O CASA

Air conditioning...Aire acondicionado
Apartment...Apartamento
Backyard...El patio
Balcony...Balcón
Bars (window)..Verjas
Bathroom..El baño

Bedroom	*El Dormitorio*
Carpeted	*Alfombrado*
Cable TV	*Telvisión por cable*
Condominium	*Condominio*
Contract	*El contrato*
Deposit	*El depósito*
Dining room	*El comedor*
Dishes	*La vajilla*
Dryer	*Secadora*
Electric bill	*Recibo de luz*
Elevator	*Elevador, ascensor*
Floor(s)	*Piso(s)*
Furnished	*Amueblado*
For rent	*Se alquila/ en alquiler*
For sale	*Se vende*
Garage	*La cochera*
Garden	*Jardín*
Ground floor	*Planta baja*
Guard	*Guarda*
Hangers	*Perchas/ ganchos*
High speed internet	*Internet de alta velocidad*
Hot water	*Agua caliente*
How do I contact the landloard?	*¿Cómo puedo localizar el casero?*
It doesn't work	*No funciona*
Key	*La llave*
Kitchen	*Cocina*
Laundry room	*Cuarto de pilas*
Living Room	*La sala*
Maid's quarters	*Cuarto de servicio*
Parking lot	*Parqueo*
Peaceful/quiet	*Tranquilo*
Refrigerator	*La refri*
Rent	*El alquiler*
Rooms	*Habitaciónes/ cuartos*

Safe	*Seguro*
Shower	*Ducha*
Shower (electric)	*Termoducha*
Stove	*Cocina*
Swimming pool	*Piscina*
Telephone	*El teléfono*
Telephone bill	*Recibo de teléfono*
Tub	*Bañera*
Unfurnished	*Sin muebles*
Utensils	*Los cubiertos*
View	*Vista*
Washing machine	*Lavadora*
Water heater	*Calentador de agua*
When do I take out the garbage?	*¿Cuándo se saca la basura?*

56. USEFUL VOCABULARY / VOCABULARIO UTIL

Are you sure?	*¿Está seguro/a?*
How	*¿Cómo?*
How much?	*¿Cuánto?*
Later	*Más tarde*
No	*No*
Now	*Ahora*
Please	*Por favor*
Thank you	*Gracias*
When?	*¿Cuándo?*
Why?	*¿Por qué?*
Where?	*¿Dónde?*
What?	*¿Qué?*
Which?	*¿Cuál?*
Yes	*Sí*
You're welcome	*Con mucho gusto/ de nada*

57. DESCRIPTION / DESCRIPCION

A little	*Poco*

A lot	*Mucho*
Above	*Arriba de*
Behind	*Detrás de*
Below	*Debajo de*
Big	*Grande*
Difficult	*Difícil*
Easy	*Fácil*
Far	*Lejos*
Fat	*Gordo/a*
Happy	*Contento/a*
Here	*Aquí*
In front of	*Delante de*
In back of	*Detrás de*
Near to	*Cerca de*
Next to	*Al lado de*
Nice/pretty	*Bonito/a*
Old	*Viejo/a*
On top of	*Encima de*
Small	*Pequeño*
There	*Allí*
Ugly	*Feo/a*
Sad	*Triste*
Short	*Bajo*
Sick	*Enfermo*
Tall	*Alto*
There	*Allí*
Thin	*Delgado*
Tired	*Cansado*
Under	*Debajo de*
Young	*Joven*

58. HANDY EXPRESSIONS / EXPRESIONES PRACTICAS

Can you help me?	*¿Puede ayudarme?*
Do you speak English?	*¿Habla usted inglés?*

Excuse me	*Perdón*
Good-bye	*Adiós*
Hurry up!	*¡Apúrese/apresúrese!*
How do you say... in Spanish?	*¿Cómo se dice en español?*
Leave me alone!	*¡Déjeme en paz!*
I've lost.	*He perdido*
I understand	*Comprendo*
I don't understand	*No comprendo*
Listen!	*¡Escuche!*
O.K.	*Está bien*
Please	*Por favor*
Please repeat	*Repita, por favor*
Wait a minute!	*¡Un momento!*
Watch out!	*¡Cuidado!*
What do you want?	*¿Qué quiere?*
What does this mean?	*¿Qué quiere decir esto?*
Where is...?	*¿Dónde está...?*

59. LEGAL TERMS / TERMINOS LEGALES

Accusation	*Denuncia*
Accused person	*Acusado*
Alimony	*Pensión alimenticia*
Appeal	*Apelación*
Appearance in court	*Comparecencia*
Bail	*Fianza*
Case	*Caso*
Civil law	*Derecho civil*
Court	*Tribunal/corte*
Court of appeals	*Corte de apelaciónes*
Criminal law	*Derecho penal*
Custody	*Patria potestad*
Defend	*Defender*
Defense attorney	*Abogado defensor*
District Attorney	*Fiscal*

Embezzlement	*Desfalco*
Eye witness	*Testigo ocular*
False witness	*Testigo falso*
Fees	*Honorarios*
Fight case	*Pelear el caso*
Fine	*Multa*
Fraud	*Fraude*
Guilt	*Culpa*
Guilty	*Culpable*
Hearing	*Audiencia*
Higher court	*Corte superior*
House arrest	*Arresto domiciliario*
Illegal	*Ilegal/prohibido*
Impediment to leave country	*Impedimento de salida*
Innocent	*Inocente*
Judge	*Juez* (masc.)/*Jueza* (fem.)
Jury	*Jurado*
Law suit	*Demanda*
Lawyer	*Abogado*
Lawyer's bar	*Colegio de Abogados*
Legal	*Legal*
Legal form	*Papel sellado*
Lower court	*Corte inferior*
Not guilty	*No culpable/absuelto*
Pleas	*Alegato*
Ruling	*Fallo*
Plaintiff	*Demandante*
Property	*Propiedad*
Prosecutor	*Fiscal/procurador*
Sentence	*Condena/sentencia*
Suit	*Demanda*
Summons	*Citación*
Take the case (lawyer)	*Llevar el caso*
Take to trial	*Llevar a juicio*

Testify.. *Declarar*
Testify against .... *Testificar/ declarar contra*
Testify for. .... *Tesitificar/ declarar a favor de...*
Trial .... *Juicio*
Try .... *Juzgar/ enjuiciar*
Verdict... *Fallo*
Will .... *Testamento*
Witness.. *Testigo*

60. BUSINESS TERMS / TERMINOS COMERCIALES

Annuity .... *Anualidad*
Asset.. *Activo*
Appraisal.. *Avalúo*
Attach assets.. *Embargar/ enganchar*
Balance of an account .... *Saldo*
Bank account .... *Cuenta*
Bank statement/statement.............................. *Estado de cuenta*
Business .... *Negocios*
Buyer... *Comprador*
C.D.s.. *Certificado de depósito*
Check... *Cheque*
Checking account.. *Cuenta corriente*
Clause.. *Cláusula*
Contract... *Contrato*
Corporation... *Sociedad*
Cost .... *Costo*
Debt .... *Deuda*
Deed.. *Escritura*
Deficit .... *Déficit*
Depreciation .... *Depreciación*
Down payment.. *Anticipo/ prima/ depósito*
Expenses/costs .... *Gastos*
Financing .... *Financiamiento*
Fair market value.. *El justo valor del mercado*

Fiscal year	*Año fiscal*
For cash	*Al contado*
Foreign exchange (hard currency)	*Divisas*
In the black/surplus of capital	*Superávit*
Income tax	*Impuesto de la renta*
Insurance	*Seguros*
Interest	*Intereses*
Interest rate	*Tasa de interés*
Investments	*Inversiones*
Land	*Terreno*
Loan	*Préstamo*
Lot	*Lote*
Money order	*Giro*
Mortgage	*Hipoteca*
Notarize	*Autenticar*
Notary	*Notario*
Parcel of land	*Parcela*
Partner	*Socio*
Pay in cash	*En efectivo*
Payments/buy on time	*A pagos*
Payment plan	*Facilidades de pago*
Price	*Precio*
Principal	*Principal*
Profitability	*Rentabilidad*
Promissory note	*Pagaré*
Property	*Propiedad*
Property taxes	*Impuestos prediales*
Record of ownership	*Registro*
Seller	*Vendedor*
Start a business	*Montar/poner un negocio*
Stock broker, real estate broker	*Corredor*
Stocks	*Acciones*
Stockholder/shareholder	*Accionista*
To subcontract/farm out	*Subcontratar*

Taxes	*Impuestos*
Tax stamps	*Timbres fiscales*
Term/period of time	*Plazo*
Transfer	*Traspaso*
To lease	*Arrendamiento*
Trust	*Fideicomiso*
Trustee	*Fideicomisario*
Value	*Valor*

61. REAL ESTATE / BIENES RAÍCES

Amortization	*Amortización*
Appraisal	*El avalúo*
Appreciation	*Apreciación*
Borrower	*El prestatario*
To borrow	*Pedir prestado*
Buyer	*El comprador*
Cash price	*Precio al contado*
Closing	*El cierre*
Collateral	*La garantía*
Clear title	*Título libre de gravámenes*
Closing cost	*Los gastos de cierre*
Compound interest	*Interés compuesto*
Contract	*El contrato*
Counter offer	*Contraoferta*
Credit rating	*El historial crediticio*
Debt	*Deuda*
Declared value	*El valor declarado*
Deed	*El título de propiedad*
Depreciation	*Depreciación/ desvalorización*
Down payment	*La prima/ pago inicial/ enganche*
Easement	*El servidumbre*
Encumbrance/lien	*El gravamen*
Equity	*El activo neto*
Extension of time	*La prórroga*

Extension of credit	*Concesión de crédito*
Farm	*La finca*
First mortgage	*Hipoteca en primer grado*
Fixed-rate mortgage	*Hipoteca con tasa de interés fija*
Fixed term	*Plazo fijo*
For sale	*En venta/ se vende*
Hall of records for property	*El registro de propiedad*
Hectare (2.5 acres)	*La hectárea*
Interest rate	*La tasa de interés*
Investment	*La inversión*
Joint tenancy	*Tenencia conjunta*
Landlord	*El casero*
Lease	*El contrato de arrendamiento*
Lender	*El prestamista*
Letter of credit	*Carta de crédito*
Line of credit	*La línea de crédito*
List price	*Precio de lista*
Loan	*El préstamo*
Market value	*El valor de mercado*
Mortgage	*La hipoteca*
To mortgage	*Hipotecar*
Offer	*La oferta*
Permit	*El permiso*
Prime interest rate	*La tasa de interés preferencial*
Property	*La propiedad/ bienes inmuebles*
Property tax	*Impuesto territorial*
Real estate	*Bienes raíces*
Real estate broker	*Corredor de bienes raíces*
Real price	*Precio real*
Rent	*El alquiler*
To rent	*Alquilar*
Second mortgage	*Hipoteca en segundo grado*
Sold	*Vendido*
Tenant	*El inquilino*

Tax	*El impuesto*
Title	*El título*
Transfer of property	*El traspaso de propiedad*
Zoning	*Zonificación*

62. EXPRESSIONS OF TIME / LA HORA

Afternoon	*Tarde*
All day	*Todo el día*
At night	*De noche*
At what time…?	*¿A qué hora...?*
At…o'clock	*A la(s)…*
Dawn	*Amanecer*
Day	*Día*
Day after tomorrow	*Pasado mañana*
Day before yesterday	*Anteayer*
Every day	*Todos los días*
In the afternoon (exact time)	*De la tarde*
In the evening (exact time)	*De la noche*
In the morning (exact time)	*De la mañana*
Midnight	*Medianoche*
Night	*Noche*
Noon	*Medio día*
On time	*A tiempo / puntual*
Sunrise	*Amanecer / Salida del sol*
Sunset	*Atardecer / Puesta del sol*
This morning	*Esta mañana*
Time (hour)	*La hora*
Today	*Hoy*
Tomorrow	*Mañana*
Tomorrow night	*Mañana por la noche*
What time is it?	*¿Qué hora es?*
Yesterday	*Ayer*
Yesterday morning	*Ayer por la mañana*

63. TELLING TIME / DECIR LA HORA

¿Qué hora es?
Son las tres.

What time is it?
It's three.

¿A qué hora?

1. ¿A qué hora cena la gente
en la Ciudad de México?
A las diez de la noche.

2.¿A qué hora cenan en los
Estados Unidos?

3. ¿A qué hora viene María a la
escuela?

4. ¿A qué hora vienen las
otras alumnas?

5. ¿A qué hora llega usted a la
su clase de Español?

6. ¿ A qué hora acaba Josué
su tarea?

7. ¿A qué hora termina la película?

8. ¿A qué hora va Juanita a su clase de Francés?

9. ¿A qué hora van al cine Teresa y Ramón?

10. ¿A qué hora llega Isabel a su casa?

¿Qué hora es?

Nueva York

Acapulco

Lima

Panamá

Ciudad de México

San José

Barcelona

PRACTICE

1. ¿Qué hora es en Barcelona?

2. ¿Qué hora es en Lima, Perú?

3. ¿Qué hora es en Acapulco?

4. ¿Qué hora es en la Ciudad de México?

5. ¿Qué hora es en Nueva York?

6. ¿Qué hora es en Panamá?

7. ¿Qué hora es en San José, Costa Rica?

Part III
The Use of Vos - The Other You

THE USE OF VOS

The Spanish spoken in Costa Rica is more or less the same as standard Castilian Spanish, except for one big difference that confuses many people. Spanish has two forms for addressing a person: *usted* and *tú*. However, in Costa Rica *vos* is used instead of *tú*. This form is seldom taught because it is considered a colloquial form. In fact, it is not found in most Spanish textbooks nor taught to most English-speaking students in their Spanish classes.

Although the use of *vos* varies from region to region, and whether it is considered standard Spanish varies widely from country to country, you can hear *vos* used in many countries in Central America, in the countries of southern South America (Chile, Argentina, Uruguay), and in parts of Colombia, Peru, and Ecuador. In parts of the Americas where there was a strong influence of the Spanish Court, places such as Mexico and Peru, the eventual change from *vos* to *tú* and *vuestra merced* to *usted* mirrored the evolution of the Spanish language in Spain. However, in regions farther away from the centers of power this evolution did not necessarily follow the same pattern.

In Costa Rica, *vos* replaces *tú* and has its own conjugation. Though it looks similar to the *tú* verbs, there are slight differences in spelling and also in stress and pronunciation. *Vos* is used only with the present indicative tense, present subjunctive, and command forms. The verb form used with vos is formed by changing the **"r"** at the end of a verb infinitive to **"s"** and adding an accent to the last syllable in the present tense. For example: *vos comprás* (comprar), *vos comés* (comer), *vos vivís*. In the present subjunctive the forms are exactly the same. For example: *vos comprés* (comprar), *vos comás* (comer), *vos vivás* (vivir). When *vos* is used in commands, just drop the final **"r"** off the infinitive ending of the verb.

For example: *comprá* (comprar), *comé* (comer), *escribí* (escribir).

MOST COMMON SET OF VERB FORMS WITH VOS

Type of verb	ending
ar	-ás
es	-és
ir	-ís

Stem changes such as **o** to **ue, e** to **ie, e** to **i**, do not occur. For certain one syllable verbs and estar, there is no difference between the tú form and the vos form (since one syllable words do not usually take accents).

For example, compare the following forms:

verb	tú form	vos form
dar	das	dás
ver	ves	vés
estar	estás	estás
ir	vas	vas

However, for most verbs there is a difference:

verb	tú form	vos form
vivir	vives	vivís
hablar	hablas	hablás
ser	eres	sos
tener	tienes	tenés
pedir	pides	pedís
construir	construyes	construís
traer	traes	traés
dormir	duermes	dormís

In most other tenses the verb forms are the same, except for the imperative vos command. That form is simply the infinitive without the **"r"** and with the vowel of the infinitive ending stressed with a written accent if it's more than one syllable or would otherwise need an accent.

verb	+ tú command	+ vos command
tener	ten	tené
ser	sé	sé
venir	ven	vení
tomar	toma	tomá
hablar	habla	hablá
vivir	vive	viví
beber	bebe	bebé
dar	da	da

Christopher Howard's World Famous Relocation and Retirement tours

Costa Rica's #1 retirement tour and the *only* retirement tour *licensed* by the Costa Rica's Tourism Institute (I.C.T.)

"The First Logical Step before Making the Move to Costa Rica"

"The tour of a lifetime."
Lani and Dan Curtis, Camarillo, California

"One of the best experiences of my life. I felt reborn."
Bill Smith, Canada

Tour with Christopher Howard, author of the best seller, **New Golden Door to Retirement and Living in Costa Rica** and *most* read authority on Costa Rica. If you are considering moving to or retiring in Costa Rica you won't want to miss this opportunity!

We offer a 6-day **Central Valley Tour** and our **popular** 9-day Combination **Central Valley and Central Pacific Beach Tour** that begin the last week of each month. These tours include a two-day highly informative seminar with the Association of Residents of Costa Rica.

You may prefer a 1, 2 or 3-day **private consultation.** No matter which you choose, you will be saving yourself time, money, and headaches by using Christopher's expertise, and having the insider tips first hand. Chris works with individuals, groups, families or couples.

Don't hesitate to call us for more information
Toll Free 800 365-2342 or visit us at **www.liveincostarica.com**
or email: **Christopher@costaricabooks.com** or **liveincostarica@cox.net**
or you can write to us at: **Live in Costa Rica Tours**
Suite 1 SJO 981, P.O. Box 025216, Miami, FL 33102-5216

Part IV

Dictionary of Tiquismos, Street Spanish, Pachuquísmos, and More

We have included this list of frequently used *tiquismos* (colloquial expressions) and *pachuquísmos*, which is a type of street dialect. The latter can be very vulgar and offensive. Some of the expressions should not be used. You will not be able to find many of these words in your standard Spanish dictionary. If you do locate any of them, they probably will not be used in the same context as in Costa Rica. Just be aware that they exist. By studying them you can better understand the native speaker.

A

Abrirse - To leave or to go
Achantado - Disappointed
Achantarse - To be lazy or not feel like doing anything
Achará - To be a pity
A culo pelado - Nude, naked
Aflojar - To pay
Agachado - Unmotivated
Agarrado - A stingy or cheap person
Agarrar cancha - To take advantage of someone or gain experience
Agarrar de chancho - To pull a person's leg or fool someone
Agarrar de maje - Make a fool of someone
Agarrar de mona - To pull someone's leg (figurative)
Agarrar el mensaje - To get the hint or idea
Agarrarse - To get into a fight
Agarrarla toda - To have good luck or success
Agarrar volados - To learn
Agazapado - Hypocrite
Agringado - To have customs and manners like a gringo
Aguado - Boring
Agüevado - Depressed or bored
Agüizote - Bad luck
Agüevarse - To become bored
Ahorcarse - To get married

Ahí nos vidrios - See you later

A la par - Next to

Al bate - To not understand something

Al trole - On foot

Alborotado - Excited (incl. sexually excited)

Alborotar el panal - Stir up things or make trouble

Alboroto - Uproar

¿Al chile? - Seriously?

Al despiste - Discretely

Alimentar las pulgas - To sleep

Algo es algo, peor son nalgas - Something is better than nothing (vulgar)

Amarrar el perro - Not to pay a debt

Amarrarse las enaguas - Act tough or impose authority (woman)

Amarrarse los pantalones - Act tough or impose authority (man)

Amarrar el perro - To pay less than one should

Armarse la gorda - To cause an uproar or start a fight

A mecate corto - On a short leash or curtail someone's freedom

A medias - To go fifty-fifty or split the cost

A medio palo - To do something halfway

A puro güevo - By force

Andar cagado en plata - To have a lot of money (vulgar)

Andar cargado - To have a lot of money

Andar con alguien - To date someone

Andar hasta el culo - To be drunk (vulgar)

Andar miado - To have bad luck

Añejo - An unkempt or dirty person

Animalada - An act caused by bad manners

Apagado - Listless person

A pata - On foot

Apenado - Embarrassed

Aperezado - Lazy

Apiar a alguien - To knock some down

Apretar - To kiss someone with passion

Apuntarse - To participate
Apurado - To be in a hurry
A puro güevo - No other choice
Argolla - A "click" or select group of people
Armarse la gorda - To start a fight
Armar un molote - To raise an uproar or cause a scene
Arrancado - To be mad or angry
Arrastrada - Woman of the streets
Arratonarse - Suffer a muscular cramp
Arriar - To hit someone
Aterro - A large amount
Arrimado - To live off someone
Atollarse - To get dirty
Atracador - A person who charges too much
Atracar - To charge too much
Atravesado - Crazy
Aventar - To rob
Aventón - To hitch a ride
Avispado - Sharp or intelligent
Avivarse - To be up to date or on top of things
Ayote, camote - Strange

B

Babosada - Stupidity
Baboso - Stupid
Bajarle el piso a alguien - To steal a person's job
Bajarle los humos a alguien - To discourage someone
Banano - Male sexual organ (vulgar)
Bandido - An astute person or rascal
Barra - Soccer fans, a bar
Barrer con todo - To take it all
Bajarse los humos - To become discouraged

Batazo - A guess
Bateador - Someone who guesses
Batear - To guess at something
Batir barro - To go off-road in a vehicle
Beneficio - A plant where coffee grains are processed
Berrinche - A temper tantrum
Bestia - A stupid person (insult)
Birra - Beer
Birrear - To drink beer
Blanco - A cigarette
Boca - An appetizer
Bochinche - A fight
Bochinchero - A fighter
Bolas - Testicles (vulgar)
Bomba - A strong mixture of liquor or type of rhyme
Bombazo - A strong alcoholic drink
Bombearse - To get drunk or bombed
Bombeta - A firecracker
Bombón - An attractive woman (vulgar)
Borona - A crumb
Botarse - To be generous
Bostezo - A boring person
Botar el rancho - To vomit
Bote - Jail
Brete - Work
Breteador - Hard working
Brochazo - Praise
Buchón - Someone who likes to "hog" things
Buenas - Good morning, good afternoon
Buena hablada - A good talker
Buena nota - A nice or cool person or thing
Bulto - A child's book bag
Burrada - A stupid act

C

Caballada - A stupid act

Caballos - Pants

Cabra - Woman, girlfriend (disrespectful)

Cabreado - Mad

Cabrearse - To become mad

Cabrón - A man (vulgar)

Cachetón - Fat cheeks

Cachos - Shoes

Caer - To visit someone

Caerle la peseta - To understand something

Cagadera - Diarrhea (vulgar)

Cagarse de risa - To laugh a lot (vulgar)

Cagarse en algo - To spoil something (vulgar)

Cagarse en alguien - To do something bad to someone (vulgar)

Cagarse en la olla de leche - To ruin something (very vulgar)

Camanance - Dimple

Camarón - A type of odd job

Camaronear - To work odd jobs

Cambiarle el agua al pajarito - To urinate (vulgar)

Camisa de once varas - A bad situation

Camote - An odd or strange person

Ser camote - To be weird

Campo - Room or space

Cantar la gallina - The woman rules the house

Cantar sin guitarra - To tell on yourself

Cañas - Slang for Costa Rican money instead of saying colones

Cañazo - Punch (hit someone)

Capearse - To escape or dodge something

Carajada - Any thing or object

Carajo - Person

Carajillo - Child

Carambada - A thing

Carbonear - To incite another person to do something

Carbonero - A person who incites others

Carebarro - A shameless person

Caer - To visit

Caripicha - Penis face (extremely vulgar)

Caripichel - Penis face (extremely vulgar)

Cartucho - Slang for the Costa Rican city of Cartago

Cascarudo - A nervy person

Un cero a la izquierda - A person who has no ability or a nobody

Cerrar el chinamo - To finish what you are doing and leave

Cerrar el pico - To shut up

Cerrar el paraguas - To die

Cien metros - One block

Cien varas - One block

Clavar el pico - To fall asleep

Clavear - To protest

Clavo - A problem

Coco - A head or shaved head

Cohete - A pistol

Colado - A person who is not invited

Colgar los tacos - To retire

Colgar los tenis - To die

Colocho - Curl (hair)

Color - Shame

Comerle a alguien - To talk bad about a person

Como alma que lleva el diablo - Do something fast

¿Cómo amaneció? - Good morning! How do you feel this morning? This expression is used to greet people only in the morning

Como entierro de pobre - To do something fast

¿Cómo está el arroz? - How is the situation?

Compa - Friend

Componerse - Change ones attitude or ways for the better
Con el moco caído - To be sad
Con toda la pata - Great, fantastic
Conchada - A gross act
Concho - A gross person
Condenado - A smart person or rascal
Con toda la pata - Perfect
Copo - Snow cone
Correrse las tejas - To go crazy
Cortarle el rabo - To fire someone from a job
Coscorrón - To hit some on the head with your knuckles
Costroso - A dirty person
Cotorra - A person who talks a lot
Creerse doña toda - To be conceited
Creerse la mamá de Tarzan - To be conceited
Cuatro ojos - A person with glasses
Cuadrar - To like something
Cuentear - To gossip or spread false rumors
Cuentero - A liar or gossip
Cuero - An ugly woman (vulgar)
Culo de tres nalgas - A conceited woman
Culo pelado - Nude (vulgar)

CH

Chances - Lottery
Chancho - A person who acts like a pig or has bad table manners
Chante - House
Chapa - A coin or stupid person
Chapear - To cut grass or brush
Chapulín - A juvenile delinquent, gang member or a tractor
Charral - A field covered with brush

Chavalo - Boy

Chavala - Girl

Chele - A person with white skin

Chepear - To snoop

Chepe - Slang for the city of San José or a nosy person

Chepito - A nosy person

Chicha - Anger or an alcoholic beverage made from fermented corn

Chicha - Also means angry

Chichero - A common alcoholic

Chichí - A baby

Chiflado - Crazy

Chile - A joke

Chinamo - A type of booth or stand usually found on the street

Chinear - To spoil or "baby" someone

Chinga - A cigarette butt

Chingar - To bother someone

Chingo - Nude

Chiripa - Coincidence or fluke

Chispa - An intelligent person

Chiva - Excellent

Chivo - A man who is supported by a woman

Cholo - A person with dark skin

Chonete - A type of hat

Chopo - A pistol

Choricear - To do illegal business or fence objects

Choricero - A person who does illegal business

Chorizo - An illegal business, scam or corruption

Chorreados - A type of pancake

Choza - House

Chozón - A big home

Chuica - A rag or old clothes

Chulear - To leach off someone or swindle

Chulo - A person who lives off others

Chumeco - A person with dark skin

Chunche - Any thing or object

Chupahuevos - An ass kisser or servile person (vulgar)

Chuzo - Car

D

Dar atole con el dedo - To string someone along

Dar bola - To flirt or pay attention to someone

Dar la talla - To do a good job

Dar pelota - To flirt or pay attention to someone

Dar vuelta - To be unfaithful to one's mate

Darle vueltas a un asunto - To toss around an idea

De buenas a primeras - Immediately

De cabo a rabo - From beginning to end

De feria - On top of that

De los once mil diablos - Big

De película - Excellent

De por sí - Anyway

De un pronto u otro - Suddenly

De viaje - All at once

Dejado - A person with an untidy appearance

Dejar botado a alguien - To stand someone up

Dejar como novia del pueblo - Means the same thing as dejar plantado

Dejar el tren - To become an old maid

Dejar plantado - To stand someone up

Dejémonos de vainas - Seriously

Desmadre - Total chaos

Despabilarse - To be on top of things

Despelote - A mess

Despiche - A mess but also can mean a "good time" or "fun"; can also mean a mess or disaster

Detrás del palo - To not understand something

¿Diay? - What can be done about it?

¡Dios guarde! - God forbid!

Dolor de culo - A pain in the butt or neck (vulgar)

Dolor de huevos - A pain in the balls or neck (vulgar)

Doña - Wife

¡Lo duda! - You said it! You are right!

E

Echado - Lazy

Echar al agua - To tell on someone; the verbs delatar, soplar or cantar are also used

Echar el caballo - Try to say nice things to seduce someone

Echar el cuento - Try to say nice things to seduce someone

Echar el ruco - Try to say nice things to seduce someone

Echarse flores - To praise oneself

Echarse la soga al cuello - To get married

Echarse un pedo - To fart (vulgar)

Echar un lance - To conquer a woman

El güevo - A lot of money

Embarcar - To put someone in a jam, involve them in something

En dos patadas - In a jiffy

En dos taconazos - In a jiffy

En un dos por tres - Quickly

Enchorpar - To put in jail

Enculado - In love (vulgar)

Enfiebrado - Enthused

Enganche - Influence

Engomado - To have a hangover

Enjaranarse - To go into debt

Enoviado - To have a boyfriend or girlfriend

Entrar con toda la valija - To be deceived by someone

En puta - A lot of something (vulgar)

Espantoso - An ugly person or thing

Está legal - It's o.k. or cool

Estaca - A cheap person

Estamos tablas - We are even (debt)!

Estañón sin fondo - A bottomless pit (appetite)

Estar bien parado - To have it made

Estar cagado - To have bad luck (vulgar)

Estar cagado en plata - To have a lot of money

Estar como todos los diablos - To be mad

Estar de buenas - To be in a good mood

Estar de buenas pulgas - To be in a good mood

Estar de chicha - To be in a bad mood

Estar de goma - To have a hangover

Estar de malas pulgas - To be in a bad mood

Estar frito - To not have a chance

Estar hasta el copete - To be fed up with something

Estar hasta el rabo - To be drunk

Estar hasta la coronilla - To be fed up with something

Estar en todas - To be well informed or on top of everything

Estar hasta el culo - To be very drunk (vulgar)

Estar hasta la mecha - To be drunk

Estar hecho leña - To bed sick, frustrated, or unmotivated

Está jodido del techo - A crazy person

Estar limpio - To be broke

Estar que se lo lleva puta - To be angry (vulgar)

Estirar la pata - To die

¡Estoy varado! - I'm stuck some place!

F

Facha - Poorly dressed

Fajarse - To work or study a lot

Fiebre - A sports fan or fanatic

Fila - A line where people wait

Filo - Hunger

Fisgonear - To snoop

Fondillo - A person's butt

Forro - A cheat sheet for an exam

Fregulo - Sick, broken or screwed up

Fregar - To bother

Fregón - A person who bothers people a lot

Fresco - A smart-ass, a drink

Fría - A beer

Fuera de onda - A person who is not up to date on things like music, clothing styles, etc.

G

Gacilla - A safety pin

Gajo - An old thing or piece of junk, worn out

Gallo pinto - Rice and beans

Garabato - Scribbling

Gastar polvo en zopilotes - Waste time on something that is not worthwhile

Gata - A jack to lift a car

Gato - A person with blue eyes

Gato encerrado - More than what meets the eye

Goma - A hangover

Greña - Unkept hair

Guaca - Money

¡Guacala! - Used to express disgust

Guachear - To spy, watch or observe

Guanaco - A person from Guanacaste (disrespectful)

Guaro - Costa Rican alcoholic sugarcane drink

Güeval - A large amount of something
Güevazo - A big hit or blow (vulgar)
Güevón - A man (said between men)
Güevonada - A stupid act
Güila - A little boy or girl
Guindo - A cliff or ravine
Guindado - Uninvited person or pest

H

Habladera - A lot of talking
Hablar en chino - To not understand
Hablar mierda - To talk a lot of crap (vulgar)
Hacerse el mae - To play dumb
Hacer ojos - To flirt
Hacer Trillo - To make a name for oneself
Hacerse el ruso - To play dumb
Harina - Money
Hasta el rabo - Drunk
Hasta la mecha - Drunk
Hecho leña - To be in bad shape
Hecho mierda - To be in bad shape (vulgar)
Hecho pistola - To be in bad shape
Hediondo - A jerk (vulgar)
Hembrón - A pretty woman (vulgar)
Hijo de puta or hijueputa - S.O.B. (vulgar)
Hijueputear - To scare or use foul language (vulgar)
Hocicón - Big mouth (disrespectful)
Hombre pendejo no goza de mujer bonita - A cowardly person won't get
     anywhere in life
Huelepedos - An ass kisser or servile person (vulgar)
Huevón - A man (vulgar)

I

Ingenio - A plant where sugar is processed
Írsele arriba a alguien - To get an advantage over someone

J

Jacha - Face
Jaibo - Stupid person (insult)
Jalado - Dissipated or pale
Jalarse una torta - To commit an error or get pregnant
Jalar - To date a person. It also means to go somewhere
¡Jale! - Hurry up! or Get moving! ("Soque" is also used)
Jama - Food
Jamar - To eat
Jamonear - To bully someone
Jamonero - Bully
Jarana - A debt
Jareta - Zipper
Jarro - Face
Jartar - To eat
Jeta - Mouth
Jetas - Studid, liar
Jetonear - To lie
Jetón - Liar
Joder - To bother (vulgar form); molestar is the correct word
Jodedera - Constant bothering of a person (vulgar)
Jodido - Difficult, sick, broken, a stubborn or evil person (vulgar)
¡No jodás! - Leave me alone! Stop bothering me! (vulgar)
¡Jueputal! - Damn! (vulgar)
Jugado - An experienced or streetwise person
Jugar de vivo - Brag or act cool

Juntado - Shacked up or living with someone
Jupa - Head
Jupa de teflón - A forgetful person
Jupón - Big headed or stubborn person

K

Kinder - Kindergarten

L

Lance - A sexual conquest
Lapicero - A ball point pen
Larguirucho - A lanky person
Lata - A bus
Leda - Age
Legal - Acceptable
Leñazo - A strong blow
Una libra - Five thousand colones (money)
Limpio - Broke

LL

Llamar a Hugo - To vomit
Llanta - A spare tire around the waist
Llevarla suave - To take it easy
Llevarse puta - To get upset (vulgar)
Llorar a moco tendido - To cry a lot

M

Macho - A person with blond hair
La madre - Terrible

Madrear - To insult a person (vulgar)

¡Mae! - A young man or stupid person

Maicero - A hick or country person (insult)

Majijo - A person who has a hair lip

Mal de patria - Homesick

Mala fama - A bad reputation

Mala ficha - A bad reputation

Mamacita - A beautiful woman (vulgar)

Mamar - To flunk a test

Mamulón - An adult or big person

¡Manda güevo! - It's unbelievable (vulgar!); how can it be?

Mandamás - The boss

Mano suelta - A person who is too generous

Manudo - A person from the city of Alajuela

Mañas - Bad habits

Maricón - Coward

Mariconada - A cowardly act

Marimba - Teeth

Matalances - A party pooper

Matar la culebra - To waste time

Me lleva puta - To be angry (vulgar)

Mear fuera del tarro - Not know what you're talking about (vulgar)

Mecha - Marijuana

Mechudo - Person with uncombed hair

Medalla - A 500 colones (Costa Rican money)

Media naranja - Your perfect mate or lover

Media teja - 50 colones (Costa Rican money)

Mentar la madre - Insult a person's mother

Mejenga - Informal pick up game of soccer

Mejenguear - To play an informal game of soccer

Meter el hombro - To help someone

Meter la pata - To put your foot in your mouth

Metiche - A nosy or nosy person

Miar - To urinate (vulgar)
Mierdoso - A brat
Moncha - Hunger
Monchar - To eat or munch
Molote - A crowd of people
Montarse en la carreta - To get drunk
Monte - Marijuana
Mover el esqueleto - To dance

N

¡Ni a palos! - Not for anything in this world
¡Ni a putas! - Not for anything in this world (vulgar)
Ni mierda - Nothing (vulgar)
¡Ni modo! - Cannot do anything about it
Ni papa - Nothing
Ni un cinco - Broke
No es jugando - Very serious
No estar en nada - To be in the dark or know anything
¡No se monte! - Don't mess with me!
¡No te atraso! - I don't care what you do!
Nota - A good thing

O

¡Ojo! - Be careful!
Olla de carne - Costa Rican stew made of meat and vegetables
Orinar fuera del tarro - Don't know what you're talking about

P

Pachanga - A party or blast
Pachuco - A type of street slang

Pachucos - Female underwear (panties)

Paco - A policeman (insult)

Paja - Lies or B.S.

Pajoso - Someone who speaks a lot of paja or B.S.

Palabrota - A vulgar word

Palanca - Pull or influence

Palenque - A thatched hut

Palmarse - To die

Palo - A tree

Palo de piso - A mop

Papero - A person who lives in Cartago

Papucho - Good looking man

Papi - Father or sweetheart

Paquetear - To deceive

Parte - Traffic or parking ticket

Pasar raspando - To scrape by on a test

Patear con los dos - Bisexual (vulgar)

Patear el balde - To kick the bucket or die

Patriarca - Foot (part of body)

Pega - A pain in the neck

Pegar el gordo - Win the lottery

Pelarse el culo - To commit an error or make a fool of oneself (vulgar)

Pegarse una ruleada - To sleep

Pelar los dientes - To smile

Pelo de gato - Drizzle

¡Pele el ojo! - Watch out!

Pelón - A party

Pelota de gente - A large group of people

Pendejada - Something of little importance

Peni - Jail

Pepiado - In love

Pepiarse - To fall in love

Perder hasta la casa santa - Lose everything.

Perder un tornillo - To be missing a screw or crazy

Perico - Cocaine

Perrear - To chase women (vulgar)

Perra - A loose woman (vulgar)

Perro - Girl crazy man

Pesado - Obnoxious

Peso - One colón (Costa Rican Money)

Pescuezo - Neck (part of the body)

Pichasear - To bat up someone (vulgar)

Piedra - Crack cocaine

Piedrero - Crack head (cocaine)

Pierna - A person of influence

Pijiarse - To get high on marijuana

Pinche - A cheap or tight-fisted person

Pichel - Face or glass pitcher

Pingüino - A nun (bad taste)

Pinta - A delinquent

Pinta - Appearance

Pinto - Rice and beans

Pipa - A smart person or coconut

Planchar la oreja - Sleep

Platero - A money

Playada - Effeminate

Playo/-a - Male/female homosexual (very offensive)

Polaco - Door-to-door salesman, a Jewish person

Polaquear - To sell from door to door

Polo - A country person or hick

Polvazal - A lot of dust

Polvo - Sex act (vulgar)

Polvazo - A person who is good in bed (vulgar)

¡Póngale! - Hurry up!

Ponerse águila - Pay attention
Ponerse al hilo - To have your bills up to date
Ponerse bravo - To get mad
Ponerse chivo - To get mad
Ponerse tapis - To get drunk
Poner como un Chuica - To humiliate
Por dicha - Fortunately
Por fa - Please
Porta a mí - Who cares?
Portrero - Pasture
Poza - Swimming hole in the river
Precarista - A squatter
Preñada - Pregnant (vulgar)
Presa - A traffic jam
Pringar - To splatter
Profe - A teacher
Pulpería - A small corner grocery store
Pulsear - To bargain or work hard
Pulseándola - Working hard
Pura mierda - Full of crap! (vulgar)
¡Pura vara! - Lies!
¡Pura vida! - Great or fantastic
Puta - Whore (vulgar)
Puros dieces - Very well
Putada - A thing (vulgar)
Putero - A whore house (vulgar)

Q

¡Qué cáscara! - What nerve!
¡Qué chiva! - How great!
¡Qué color! - How embarrassing!

Quedado - Someone who flunks the school year

Quedar como un culo - Look like a fool (vulgar)

Quedarse - To flunk in school

Quedarse como misa - To be silent

Quedarse en la calle - To go broke

¡Qué dicha! - Good!

¿Qué es la vara? - What's going on?

¡Qué madre! - What a drag!

¿Qué me dice? - How's it going?

¡Qué pelada! - How embarrassing!

¡Qué pereza! - What a drag!

Queque - Something that is easy or as we say "a piece of cake"

¡Qué rico! - How good (food, woman, etc.)

¡Qué rollo! - What a pity!

¡Qué tirada! - What a problem, pity!

¡Qué torta! - What a mess!

¡Qué va! - No way!

Quitado - A boring person

Quitarse el tiro - To avoid a responsibility

R

Rabo - A person's rear end

Regalar - To have a baby

Rajar - To brag

Rajón - A bragger

Rancho - House

Rancho - Vomit (vulgar)

Rata - A bad person

Rayar - To pass another car on the street

Regar bolas - To spread gossip

Regarse - To have an orgasm (vulgar)

Regar la bola - To spread the word
Regar las bilis - To get mad or irritated
Reguero - A mess
Reputiar - To insult (vulgar)
Reventada - A good looking woman
Ricura - Pleasant
Robar pasto - Steal someone's mate
Roco - An old person
Rocolo - An old person
Rocola - A juke box
Rodar - To deceive by stringing along
Rogelio - A 1000 colón bill
Rojo - A 1000 colón bill
Ruco - Horse or pants
Ruliar - To sleep

S

Sacarse el clavo - To avenge
Sacarle el jugo a algo - Take advantage of a situation
¡Salado! - Tough luck! Person with bad luck
Salvada - Any action that gets you out of a jam
Salvar - To get someone out of a jam
Salveque - A backpack
Salir aventado - Quickly
Salvar la tanda - To get out of a jam
Samueleador - A Peeping Tom
Samuelear - To spy on
Sancochar - To steam vegetables
Sangrón - Bully
Sapear - To accuse
Sapo - A tattle tale

Sátiro - A dirty old man

Se la juega - Know how to handle or manage something

Se les da la mano y cogen el codo - Give them an inch and they will take a mile

Semerendo - Anything that is big

Ser buena nota - To be a "cool" person

Ser codo - A cheap person

Ser como carne y uña - To be good friends

Ser pipa - To be intelligent

Serruchar el piso - To back stab someone

Sinvergüenzada - A shameless act

Sobársela - To masturbate (vulgar)

Soda - A small luncheonette

Socado - Fast

Soplarse - To hurry

¡Soque! - Hurry up!

Sordina - Deaf

¡Suave! - Take it easy!

Subirse el apellido - To get mad

Subírsele el humo a la cabeza - Something goes to someone's head
    like their success, etc.

Subírsele el apellido - To get mad

Sudar la gota gorda - To work hard

T

Tallado - Broke, no money

Tamaño poco - A lot

Tanda - A drinking binge

La tapa del perol - The best of the best

Tapia - Deaf

Tapis - A drink of liquor or to be drunk

Tarreado - Drunk

Tarro - Jail (slang)

Tata - Father

Te conozco mosco - To know someone well

Teja - A 100 colón bill

Tener buena cuchara - To be a good cook

Tener hasta el copete - To be fed up with something

Tener la papa en la mano - Have something easy

Templado - A person who gets sexually aroused easily

Templarse - Get sexually excited (vulgar)

Tener chicha - To be angry

Tener chispa - To be intelligent

Tener todo el güevo - To a have a lot of money

Tico - A Costa Rican

Tigra - Laziness

Tieso - Broke or not having money

Timba - A fat stomach

Tiquicia - Costa Rica

Tiro - Solution.

Tombo - A policeman

¡Tome chichi! - Take that!

Torcido - Bad luck

Tortero - A person who gets into a lot of problems or causes them

Tortuguismo - A work "slow down"

Tostado - Drugged or crazy

Tragársela - To believe a lie

Trolear - To walk or go on foot

Tramo - A type of stand used by street vendors

Trillo - A path

Troles - Your feet

Trompa - Mouth

Tuanis - Great, Nice, or Fantastic

Tucán - A 5000 colón bill

¡Tumba la vara! - Stop bothering me
Turistear - To travel

V

Vacilón - Fun
Vacilar - To joke or have fun
Vaina - A thing
Vara - A thing or object
Varas - Just kidding
Vararse - To have your car break down
Veranillo de San Juan - Indian Summer
Vergazo - A blow or hit (vulgar)
Vergear - To beat someone (vulgar)
Verla fea - To be in a jam
Vieja de patio - A gossip
Viejo verde - A dirty old man
Vieras - You should have seen
Vino - A nosy person.
Vinear - To snoop
Vivazo - An astute or sharp person
Volar - To fire a person
Volar pico - To talk
Volar pata - To walk
Volar plomo - To shoot
Vos - Familiar form used to address people in Costa Rica instead of tú
Vuelta - An errand
Vuelto - Change (money) from a transaction
Vueltón - A long distance or trip

W

Wachiman - A guard or watchman

Y

Ya vengo - I will be right there
Ya voy - I will be right there
¿Idiay? - What is the problem?
Yodo - Coffee
Yunta - A couple (people)
Yuyo - A person who bothers you a lot or a pest

Z

Zaguate - A mutt, street dog or a womanizer
Zapatero a sus zapatos - Get to work!
Zaradajo - Old clothes or rags
Zarpe - The last drink or one for the road
Zocar - To hurry
Zompopa - A big ant
Zorra - A lose woman (vulgar)
Zorro - A girl crazy man (vulgar)
Zorrear - To look for women (vulgar)

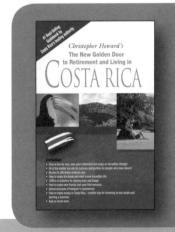

Part V
Costa Rican Proverbs and Sayings

Although most of the expressions below are used only in Costa Rica, some are also utilized in other Latin American countries and in Spain.

A

A buen diente no hay mal pan - Not to decline help when you are in need of something.

A Cartago hay que ir a enterrar un pariente o cobrar una herencia - You go to Cartago (Costa Rica) only go to bury someone or to cash an inheritance.

A todo trapo - Full speed.

A brincos y a saltos - Difficulty.

A caballo regalado no se le mira el colmillo - Beggars can't be choosers.

A calzón quitado - To do something openly.

A casa de nadie ninguno va, porque solo uno sabe como cada uno está - Everyone knows their own affairs.

A comer y a misa solamente una vez se avisa - Some things are only told once.

A cómo come el mulo caga el culo - The size of the poop is according to how much the mule eats (consequences are the result of your actions).

A cómo es el chico es la vaca; a como es el sapo es la pedrada - Problems are dealt with according to their size.

A costillas de - To live or mooch off someone.

A Dios rogando y con el mazo dando - Pray to God but keep laboring.

A dos carriles - Working at full speed.

A dos sogas no hay toro bravo - Approach something from all angles.

A ese paso nunca va a amanecer - Better put a move on things.

A falta de pan, buenas son tortas; A falta de polla, pan y cebolla - When things are scarce, anything will do.

A gato viejo ratón tierno - Old men who like to run with younger women.

A golpe dado no hay quite - Somethings are inevitable.

A hierro ardiente, martillo batiente - All work has to be approached with effort.

A la brava - To be forced to do something.

A la cuarta ni los bueyes - The fourth attempt is hard.

A la fuerza ni los zapatos entrar - People don't like to do things they are forced into doing.

A la par del chorro y muerto de sed; A la par del mar sin poderse bañar - Unable to see a clear solution to a problem.

A la pura bulla - Just like that!.

A la quinta es la vencida - After five times, we give up.

A la tercera va la vencida - Third time is a charm.

A lo hecho pecho - Forget the past.

A lo malo nadie se acostumbra - No one gets used to bad luck.

A lo que estamos, tuerta; A lo que te truje, Tencha - Let´s do what we came here to do.

A los bueyes nuevos llamarlos por delante - It is better to be leery of the inexperienced.

A los perros solo una vez los capan - Dogs are castrated only once (people should learn from past mistakes).

A mal tiempo buena cara - In the face of adversity stay calm.

A mecate corto - To have someone on a short leash.

A mí con flores siendo yo de Heredia - Not to be tricked as easily.

A nadie le amarga un dulce; A nadie le disgusta un confite - A sweet never sours the spirit.

A nadie le caen las hojas del cielo pa´que haga los tamales - Nothing is achieved without effort.

A ojos cerrados - To do something without thinking about it.

A otra cosa, mariposa - Let´s change the subject.

A otro perro con ese hueso - Go tell it to the Marines.

A palabras necias oídos sordos - Don't pay attention to stupid things people say.

A pájaro manso, la puerta abierta - There are some things (or persons) we can trust.

A pan duro diente agudo - Put on a good face to hardships.

A paso de carreta - To do something slowly.

A paso de tortuga - At a snail's pace.

A pellizcos muere el burro - You have to persevere to achieve a goal.

A puñalada por bollo de pan - Hard economic times/personal finances.

A puro huevo - With a lot of effort.

A quien de ajeno se viste, las costuras le hacen llagas - Better to keep to oneself.

A quien le duele la muela que se la saque - You have to solve your own problems.

A raja tablas - Fast.

A rey muerto, rey puesto - There is always someone to take your place.

A rienda suelta - Freely without restrictions.

A su tiempo maduran las uvas - There is a time for everything.

A todo chancho gordo le llega su día - Everyone gets what the have coming to them.

A todo dar - To be doing well.

A todo gallinero llega el zorro - Bad things can happen to anyone.

A todo perro flaco se le pegan las pulgas - A lot of bad things happen to people who are already unfortunate.

A todo "se hace" uno - One gets used to everything.

A un vagazo poco caso - Don't pay attention to people you hold in low regard.

A uno no se lo roban para no mantenerlo - Some people will steal you blind.

A veces es peor el remedio que la enfermedad - Sometimes the cure is worse than the disease.

A ver si como ronca duerme - To back up one's words with actions.

Abrir un hueco para tapar otro - Try to fix one mistake but commit another error in the process.

Acabar la cuerda - To stop talking.

Acabar la teta - To stop reaping the benefits from something.

Acatar - To think or realize.

Acostarse con las gallinas - To go to sleep early.

Adelante como el elefante - To encourage a person to do something.

Aflojar el pollo - To spend money.

Agacharse la cabeza - To be humiliated.

Agarrar de chancho - To deceive.

Agarrar dos panales en el mismo palo - To accomplish two things at the same time.

Agarrar la onda - To understand something.

Agarrar la vara - To bother someone.

Agarrarle a alguien con las manos en la masa - To catch someone in the act or red handed.

Aguantar la burra - To put up with something.

Aguanta más que un zorro - Strong person, tough to beat.

Aguar la fiesta - To be a kill-joy or party pooper.

¡Al agua patos! - Let´s do it!.

Al buen peón siempre lo llaman - Good workers are always sought after.

Al buey por el cacho y el hombre por la palabra; Al buey por el cacho y al hombre por el bigote - To trust a man on the basis of his gentleman´s word.

Al César lo que es del César - Giving credit to someone when well deserved.

Al chancho con lo que lo crían - If raised as a pig, always be a pig.

Al hombre le entra el amor por los ojos y la mujer por los oídos - Love enters through the eye and women through the ear (love can be tricky).

Al ladrón las llaves - To confide in person of dubious reputation.

Al lobo viejo, carne fresca - Older men like younger women.

Al mejor espía nadie lo conoce - Beware of people who are hard to tell.

Al mejor mono se le cae el zapote - Anyone can make mistakes.

Al que no lleva la carga le parece que no pesa - Loads are not heavy for the one not carrying it.

A novilo bravo, a la raíz del cacho - A serious problem should be faced immediately.

Al pan, pan, al vino, vino - Tell things like they are.

Al que a buen árbol se arrima, buena sombra la cobija - If you hang around with successful people it will rub off on you.

Al que de ajeno se viste, en la calle lo desvisten - Robbers will be robbed.

Al que Dios se la da San Pedro se la bendice - If God gives it, Saint Peter bless it.

Al que le cae el guante que se lo plante - Have to face the consequences.

Al que madruga dios le ayuda - To be successful you have to get up early in the morning.

Al que madruga come pechuga - Means the same as the last entry.

Al que no quiere caldo, dos tazas - To be forced to do something you don´t like a number of times.

Al que no tiene luz propia, lo deslumbran los faroles - If you don´t excel on your own, you´ll be impressed by the ones who do.

Al que se presta el Diablo lo tienta - If you ask for it, you´ll get it.

Al tonto ni Dios ni el Diablo lo quieren - Fools are disliked by God and the devil.

Alborotar el panal - To stir things up or cause problems.

Alborotar la tripa - To make someone hungry.

Alegrón de burro - A happy reaction to great news that aren´t true.

Algún día todo se acaba: everyting will come to the end.

Alimentar las pulgas - To sleep.

Alzar a uno el rabo - To help someone.

Amar un broncón de los once mil - To cause a big problem.

Amarrar el perro - Not to pay a debt.

*Amarrase los pantalone*s - To act with vigor.

Amor con hambre no dura - Economic problems can ruin a relationship.

Andar a puro chinge - A hardy type person.

Andar buscando sarna para poder rascarse - To look for trouble.

Andar con caites de lata - To leery about a situation.

Andar cargado - To be loaded with money.

Andar como el pizote solo - To be alone.

Andar como judío errante - To be wander around.

Andar como lora en mosaico - To walk carefully for fear of slipping.

Andar como Pedro por su casa - To act like one owns the place.

Andar como perro sin dueño - Wander around aimlessly.

Anda como pisote solo - a lonely person.

Andar como un chancho - Unkept, dirty.

Andar como un rifle viejo, dispuesto a cualquier desgracia - Someone willing to try anything.

Andar con el moco caído - To be depressed or down.

Andar con la cara en glorias y el culo en penas - Looks are deceiving.

Andar con la procesión por dentro - To keep things bottled in.

Andar con pies de plomo - To move slowly.

Andar de arrecostado - To live off someone.

Andar de Bagaces a Liberia - (Costa Rica) idle, going from one place to another.

Andar de la Ceca a la Meca; Andar del timbo al tambo - To go from one place to another.

Anda de moscón - Interferring with a couples´s privacy.

Andar de tanda - To get drunk.

Andar (alguien) oreja de mula con uno - To be on the lookout with someone.

Andar en facha - To dress badly.

Andar en órbita - To be drugged.

Andar midiendo calles - To wander around.

Andar pajareando - To waste time.

Ando yo caliente, ríase la gente - If it doesn´t pertain me, doesn´t affect me.

Apagar el puro - To disappoint someone.

Apenado - To be ashamed.

Aquí el que no cae resbala - A difficult situation to get out of it.

Aquí hay un gato encerrado - There is more than meets the eye.

Argolla - A click or group of select people.

Arrieros somos y en el camino andamos - Our life is predestined.

Arrímale una naranjita agria para abrirle el apetito - A sour orange opens the appetite.

Arrollar los petates para el otro barrio - To roll over and die.

Así como es el chancho es la horqueta - The size of the pig determines its harness.

Atizar la hoguera - To stir up trouble.

Aunque comas flores lo que cagas es mierda - We poop just like everybody else no matter who we are.

Aunque la jaula sea de oro, no déja de ser prisión - A gold cage is nevertheless a prison.

Aunque la mona se vista de seda, mona se queda - It's hard to change who you are by changing your appearance.

Aunque la mula sea mansa, alguna maña le queda - Old habits are hard to break.

Aventarse de la casa - to change residency very suddenly.

Ay de los hombres ingratos que andan de noche como los gatos - Beware of men who. just like cats, like the night (some men are unfaithful by nature).

Ayúdate, que Dios te ayudará - Help yourself and God will help you.

B

Bagaces (Guanacaste) es el único pueblo que tiene una entrada y siete salidas - Bagaces (Guanacaste) has more exits than entrances

Báilame esa mona en la uña - Say that again!

Bailar con la más fea - To be in a troublesome situation

Bailar en una pata - To be happy

Bajar la marea - The problem or trouble is over

Bajarse de las nubes - To come down to earth or face reality

Bajársele la cresta - To learn to be humble after a hard lesson

Barba de tres colores, esa es barba de traidores - Beware of man with a three-colored beard

Barco parado no gana flete - If you don't work you won't get paid or make money

Barril sin fondo - A bottomless pit or someone who has a big appetite

Barva oscuro, aguacero seguro - Barva Volcano (Costa Rica,) cloudy in the morning, rainy in the afternoon

Bien ama quien nunca olvida - Love a lot who doesn´t forget

Boda y mortaja del cielo bajan - Marriage and death seem predestined

Borracho que come miel ¡que Dios se apiade de él - Beware of a drunkard who likes honey

Borrón y cuenta nueva - To forget the past and start with a clean slate

Botar el tapón - To release your anger

Buen abogado, mal cristiano - Good lawyer, not a good Christian

Bueno le dijo la mula al freno, que entre más grande más bueno - To conclude a project and feel good about it

Buey sólo bien se lame: - Lonely person looks after himself

Buscar hueso - To look for a job

Buscar río arriba el ahogado - To look for things in the wrong place

Buscarle la comba al palo - To find a way to solve something

C

Caballo con la rienda, mujer con la espuela - Handle the horse with the reins and the women with the spurs

Caballo grande, aunque no ande - Bigger is not always better

Caballo viejo no cambia el paso - It is hard to change an old habit

Cacarear y no poner huevo - All talk

Cada abeja a su panal; Cada cosa con su cosa; Cada cual es cada cual; Cada jumo con su guaro - To each its own

Cada cabeza es un mundo - Everyone thinks differently

Cada chancho en su chiquero - Each pig to its own sty

Cada gallo en su patio - People feel better in their own surroundings

Cada guila nace con su tortilla bajo el brazo - Nature provides everyone what we need

Cada ladrón juzga por su opinion - People judge others according to their own behavior

Cada loco con su tema - To each his own

Cada loro en su estaca - Each parrot to its own perch

Cada muerte de obispo - Almost never

Cada oveja con su pareja - People should hang out with other people who have the same position in life

Cada palo aguanta su vela - People must be responsible for their acts

Cada quien en su casa y Dios en la de todos - Everyone is king in their own house

Cada quien sabe donde le aprieta el zapato - Everyone knows where the shoe rubs

Cada quien tiene su modo de matar pulgas - Everybody has their own way to do things

Cada uno en su casa y dios en la de todos - Don't get involved in other people's business

Cada uno tiene su modo de matar pulgas - People have their own way of doing things

Candil de la calle, oscuridad de la casa - Hypocrite

Caer como un plátano - To get to bed exhausted

Caer como San Juan al 24 - Something happening on a very opportune time (San Juan´s festivities in Costa Rica are on June 24th)

Cambiar la mamá por un burro - To make a bad deal

Candil de la calle, oscuridad de la casa - An example to others but an annoyance at home

Carro de pobre, pobre carro - Car owned by a pauper, poor car (when things are not well taken care of)

Casa la que tengas y plata la que podas - Be glad with the house and money you have

Casa y mujer nunca se acaban de componer - House and wife always need upgrading

Casarse es bonito, lo feo es estar casado - Marriage is nice, bad is to be married to someone

Cerdo pero no trompudo - In bad shape, but not that bad

Cinco lampiños no hacen un barbudo - It takes a lot to make something really good

Coger el rábano por las hojas - To approach a problem right away

Colgarle el guecho - A gullible person

Coman bastante, que no soy el que paga - Eat a lot, I am not paying the bill!

Come santos y caga diablos - A churchgoer that is not virtuous

Como calabazo en remolino, que ni se hunde, ni hace camino - Someone who is in the way

Como cuando usted era pobre - I´m fine, just like when you used to be poor!

Como el que tiene hambre y le dan bicarbonato - Sometimes we get what we don´t want

Como entierro de pobre - Walk or do something very fast

Como primo me le arrimo - You can always count on family

Como soplar y hacer botellas - A task that is easy to accomplish

Como trapito de dominguear - Spiffy, any project to be proud of

Con abono, lluvia y tractor, cualquier pendejo es agricultor - Not every fool can work the land

Con la pata en el estribo, muchos se quedan colgando - There are people who are just hanging in there

Con ladrones y gatos, pocos tratos - Be leery when dealing with dishonest people

Con todo al viento – Naked

Con paciencia y esperanza el cielo se alcanza - With patience you can reach the heavens

Con paciencia y saliva un elefante se comió una hormiga - With enough patience everything is achieved

Con velo y corona y el culo como una mona - Some women appear pure but they are not

Cortados con las mismas tijeras - Birds of a feather or two people who are alike

Coyol comido, coyol quebrado - To live form day to day

Coyol partido, coyol comido - To struggle financially (same as the last entry)

Crecer como el rabo de las vacas (para abajo) - To grow the other way (downwards)

Cría cuervos y te sacan los ojos - If you help ungrateful pople they won't repay you

Cría fama, échate a dormir - It's easy to lose all that you've gained

Cuando el río suena, piedras trae - Life gives us warnings

Cuando el saco se menea algo tiene adentro - If it moves it is because something is inside

Cuando el viaje es corto cualquier yegua es buena aunque sea renca - If the trip is short, any old lame mule will do

Cuando la pedrada esta pa´l perro ni que se meta debajo de la cama - When something is meant for you, there is no stop to it

Cuando la rana echa pelos - An impossible situation or something that will never happen

Cuando las purrujas pican me rasco - If it is my problem, I´ll take care of it

Cuando las ratas abandonan el barco es porque se va a hundir - When messages come your way is better to pay attention

Cuando llueve todos nos mojamos - Misfortune doesn´t discriminate

Cuando menos se espera salta la liebre - Things happen when you least expect it

Cuando no hay lomo de todo como - When hunger strikes everything is appetizing

Cuando salgas no lleves hamaca, ni guitarra ni mujer - If want a good time, better leave your hammock, guitar and wife behind

Cuando se corta un árbol todas sus ramas se caen - When a tree falls, all its branches die (take care not to destroy something useful)

Cuando una está salado hasta los perros lo mean - To have bad luck

Cuando una puerta se cierra, otra se abre - When a door closes, another one opens up

Cuando uno piensa, llega la pelona - Death can come at anytime

Cuando uno está de malas, hasta los perros lo mean - When one is unlucky, everything ends up bad

Cuando uno quita la piedra se acaban los trompezones - When the stone is removed, so is the obstacle

Cuando uno se encuentra un huevo, es güero - Things that are not found easily aren´t always good

Cuando veas que le cortan las barbas al vecino, pone las tuyas a remojar - Your neighbords´problems can also affect you

Cucharita, cucharetas, donde no te llaman, no te metas - Mind your own business

Cuentas claras chocolate espeso - To have paid off a debt or be even

Culo sentado no gana bocado - If you sit on your butt, you won't make any money

Cuñadas en paz y juntas, solo difuntas - Sisters in-law can hardly get along

CH

Chancho limpio nunca engord - Don´t be so picky

Chivo expiatorio - Scapegoat

Chupar sal fuera del saco - To look at a problem from the outside

D

Dar agua a los caites - To run like heck

Dar atole con el dedo - To string somebody alone or deceive them

Dar en el blanco - Hit the nail on its head

Dar la talla - To meet all expectations

Dar los veinte - To end a romantic relationship

Dar más vueltas que un perro sin sueño - To be restless

Dar pelota - To flirt with someone

Dar sopa de muñeca - To whip someone

Dar el campanazo - To give a warning

Dar una puntada a tiempo y te ahorraras ciento - A stitch in time saves nine

Dar vuelta a la hoja - To change the subject of a conversation when talking

Darse aires - To brag

Darse con una piedra en el pecho - Be grateful for what you have

De buenas intenciones está empedrado el camino al infierno - To seek out justifications for your actions

¿De dónde telas si no hay arañas? When things are scarce

De dos torcidos se hace un torzal - Two unlucky people make lots

De esos que no comen miel escondo yo mi jicote: - Be careful with the virtuous ones

De la mano a la boca se pierde la sopa; De mano en mano se perdió una vaca - Watch out for rip offs

De las aguas mansas, líbrame Dios - God save me from the meek

De dos males, el menor - The lesser of the two evils

De la calle vendrá quien de la casa te echará - Be aware of so-called friends that might kick you out from your own home

De la lagartija para arriba todo es cacería - Everything is fair game in love

De los arrenpetidos se sirve Dios - God likes those who repent

De los dientes para afuera - To be insincere

De noche todos las gatos son pardos - In the dark it is hard to see someone's defects

De pocas pulgas - Someone with a short fuse

De por sí la calavera es ñata - Things are the way they are

¿De qué arteria sale esta sangre? Where did this one come from?

De tal palo, tal astilla - Like father like son, etc.

De tanto lamer el perro saca sangre - It is not always good to persist on the same thing

De un solo tiro - Once and for all

De viaje - Completely

Debajo de las cascaras están los alacranes - Watch out for what you don´t see plainly

Debajo de las cobijas se arreglan las cosas - Most marriage problems don't last

Decir yeguadas - To speak nothing but stupidities

Dejar a uno el tren - Someone who doesn't get married or misses the boat

Dejar a uno guindado - To leave someone waiting

Dejar carne asando - To be in a hurry

Dejar enterrado el ombligo - To miss the place your belly button was buried (to miss home)

Dejó frijoles cocinando - Someone in a big hurry

Dejar las pulgas en otra parte - To leave or go away

Dejar los pelos en el alambre - To escape by when something is difficult

Del dicho al hecho hay mucho trecho - Easier said than done

Del mismo cuero salen las correas - The expenses should be deducted from the earnings

Desconfiar de su propia sombra - To not trust your own shadow

Desnudar a un santo par vestir a otro - To rob Peter to pay Paul

Despacio y con buena letra - To do things slowly so they turn out well

Destaparse el tamal - Discover something bad or all hell broke loose

Dichosos los que tienen tata rico y patrón macho - Some people have it better than others

Dime con quien andas y te diré quien quien eres - Birds of a feather flock together

Dios aprieta pero no ahoga - God squeezes but does not drawn you

Dios lo oiga y el Diablo se haga el sordo - May God forgives them

Dios los hace and el Diablo los junta - God creates them and the devil bring them together

Dios no da alas a animal ponzoñoso - God does not give feathers to poisonous creatures

Dios tarda pero no olvida – God doesn't forget

Doblar el codo - To get drunk

Doblar el espinazo - To work

Donde canta la gallina está el huevo - When the hen calls, there is an egg

Donde ese gallo canta ningún pollo cacarea - The weaklings can´t challenge the strong

Donde fueres haz como vieres - When in Rome do as the Romans

Donde hay amor hay celos - Where there is love, there is jealousy

Donde hay fuego sale humo - Where there is fire, there is smoke

Donde manda el capitán, no manda marinero - You have to obey your superiors

Donde menos se piensa salta la liebre - The hare jumps in the least expected place
   (things sometimes happen unexpectedly)

Donde no hay harina todo se vuelve torremolina - Poverty is cause of many problems

Donde se llora, está el muerto - Used for people who have no reason to complain

Donde ronca el tigra no hay burro paralítico - When there is danger everyone
   runs from it

Dos son tres - Where there is room for two, there is also room for three

Donde todos mandan nadie obedece - When everybody is boss, nobody obeys

Dorar la píldora - To coat a pill with sugar (figurative)

Dormir a pierna suelta - To sleep well

Dormir con un ojo abierto - To be alert

Dormirse en los laureles - Don't rest on your laurels

Dos cabezas piensan mejor que una - Two heads think better than one

Dura más una saliva en la plancha de un sastre - Something that is short living

E

Echando a perder se aprende - Practice makes perfect

El agua cuando llega al pellejo, escurre - Problems can be shaken off at their due time

Echar al agua - To tell on someone

Echar carbón - To pit one person against another

Echar chispas - To be mad

Echar el hombro - To help someone

Echar el resto - To stay with the ones you want

Echar en cara - To remind someone what you have done for them

Echar en su saco - To benefit from a lesson learned

Echar la chayotera - To put your signature on something

Echarle la pierna a un caballo; Echarse al plan - To mean business

Echar patas - To disappear or get robbed

Echar raíces - To stay a long time in one place

Echarle el churuco a alguien - To put the blame on someone else

Echarle maíz la pava - To brag

Echarse (lo) al bolsillo - Something easy to do; easy as pie

Echarse a la calle - To become a prostitute

Echarse la soga al cuello - To get married

Echase una cana al aire - To have a good time

El ayer es el ayer y el hoy es el hoy - Is better to live in the present

El bien de los más puede ser el mal de los menos - The good of some can be the bad of others

El buey lerdo se bebe el agua sucia - The person who arrives last gets served last

El buey sólo bien se lame - When living alone one learns to be independent

El burro adelante para que no se espante - Someone who puts themselves first when talking

El burro no pisa por lo lindo sino por lo necio - Refers to the stubborn

El camino malo hay que andarlo ligero - Learn to get rid of your troubles quickly

El chancho es blanco pero la morcilla es negra - The pig is white, but its blood isn´t (something in the outside may appear to be good)

El casado casa quiere - Newly married wants new home

El comal le dice a la olla □ culo quemaő □ ; El sartén le dice a la olla □ cuidao me quemas□ - It is hard for people to find their own faults

El comal le dice a la olla, quitate porque me atollas: - The skillet tells the pot: don´t rub me with your soot (someone who criticizes others despite their own faults)

El cura no se acuerda de cuando fue monaguillo - We don´t remember the times we were down

El diablo hace las ollas pero no las tapas - The devil creates trouble but not the solutions

El frio sabe a dónde se arrima - Trouble knows its own company

El fuego quema y el amor también - Fire burns and so does love.

El gallo fino canta en su corral y en el del vecino - Good traits are good everywhere

El gato miaullador no es buen cazador - Tooting your horn doesn´t make you good

El golpe avisa y el chichote enseña - The blow makes you aware

El guaro es la leche de los viejos - Old folks sometimes can find solace on alcohol

El guaro no se hizo para lavar maíz - Liquor is making for drinking

El guaro suelta la lengua y amarra las manos - Alcohol loosen your tongue but tie your hands

El hábito no hace al monje - You have to look at what is inside people to see what they are really like

El hilo revienta por lo mas delgado - The thread breaks on the thinnest point

El hombre es como el oso, mientras más feo, más hermoso - Ugly man, is an attractive man

El hombre es el único animal que tropieza dos veces con la misma piedra - Man is the only animal that repeats the same mistakes

El hombre propone y Dios dispone - Man proposes but God decides

El hombre propone y la mujer dispone - In matters of love, man proposes y women decide

El lomo ajeno aguanta más - Loads carried by others seem lighter

El matrimonio es una lotería - Marriage is like the lottery

El mejor pleito es el que no se hace - In a fight, everyone loses

El mono sabe a que palo se trepa - It is important to learn to discrimínate

El muerto está vivo mientras empañe el vidrio - Have to fight until the end

El pez gordo se come al chico - Big fish eat little fish

El ojo de amo engorda el ganado - A boss should mindful of the shop

El ojo del amo engorda la cabalgadura - A boss should mindful of the shop

El pájaro canta aunque la rama cruja - Things happen when they have to happen

El papel aguanta lo que le pongan - Paper can take anything you write on it

El pato se conoce entre las gallinas - A duck is known among the chickens

El peor chanco se lleva la mejor mazorca - The least deserving people get the best things

El peor intento es el que no se hace - The worst effort is the one not attempted

El poderoso caballero es don dinero - Money is power

El que a hierro vive a hierro muere - He who lives by the sword dies by the sword

El que anda con lobos aullar aprende - Birds of a feather flock together

El que busca encuentra -He who seeks finds

El que calla otorga - He who doesn't say anything gives tacit approval

El que canta, su mal espanta - To put a happy face in the midst of difficulties

El que canta su mal espanta y el que llora su mal emperora - Putting in a good face to rough times

El que con niños se acuesta mojadito amanece - Stay away from the ones who can get you in trouble

El que con tigre se acuesta, desplumado amanece - If you court trouble, you´ll find trouble

El que cria perro ajeno, pierde el pan y pierde el perro - You can get in trouble when taking care of others´property

El que da primero, da dos veces - He who strikes first, hits twice.

El que da y quita se vuelve cuita - An Indian Giver

El que es torcido donde quiere pierde - When unlucky you are unlucky everywhere

El que ha de ser olote, aunque el aguacero sea copioso - When destined to be one way that is the way it will be

El que la debe la teme - When free of sin, free of fear

El que le hace un favor al diablo con llevárselo le paga - to repay a good action with a bad deed

El que es mandado no es culpado: - The one obeying orders cannot be blamed

El que es perico dondequiera es verde y el que es torcido dondequiera pierde - Bad luck will follow unlucky people

El que madruga come pechuga - It's good to start the day early

El que más tiene, más quiere - The one who has the most, want the most

El que mucho abarca, poco aprieta - He has too much ambition ends up with nothing

El que mucho corre, pronto para - The quicker you run, the sooner you stop

El que mucho escoge, lo peor se lleva - If you are too picky you end up with the worst

El que mucho habla, mucho yerra - The one who talk the most, make the most errors

El que nace para tamal, del cielo le caen las hojas: - If destined to be a corn cake (tamal), heaven will send you the wrappers

El que nace para maceta del corredor no pasa - If destined for flower pot, from the corridor won´t be budged

El que nace para burro del cielo le caen las orejas - If destined to be a burro, heaven will send you ears

El que nació para necio, el diablo le tiene aprecio - Stubborness will get in the way

El que nada debe, nada teme - He who doesn't owe anything has nothing to fear

El que no llora no mama - You have to protest or complain to get something

El que no nada se ahoga - If you don´t swim, you may drown

El que no quiera decepciones que no se haga de ilusiones - False illusions, big frustrations

El que no quiere ver bultos, que no salga a la calle - Stay at home if you want to avoid problems

El que no sabe pedir, no sabe vivir - He who doesn´t ask, doesn´t receive

El que no se arriesga no pasa el río - You have to chances to get something in life

El que no se echa al agua, no pasa al río - You have to take the plunge achieve something

El que no tiene dinga tiene mandinga - If it's not one thing it's another

El que no tiene plata, no tiene amigos - No money, no friends

El que no vive para servir no sirve para vivir - He who doesn´t serve, doesn´t know how to live

El que nunca ha visto altares en cualquier horno viejo se persina - When not accustomed to riches, everything looks grand

El que parte y reparte le toca la mayor parte - He who cuts the cake gets the biggest slice

El que pega primero pega dos veces -He takes the initiative has an advantage

El que pestañea pierde - You lose in the battling of an eye

El que por su gusto muere que lo entierren de a parado - People who choose to die don´t deserve a good burial

El que puede, puede - The one who can, can

El que puede puede, y el que no, esta jodido - The one who can, can, and the one who can´t is a loser

El que quiere camarones, que se moje los calzones -If you want something you have to work for it

El que quiere celeste que le cueste - There is no such thing as a free lunch

El que ríe de último, ríe mejor - He, who laughs last, laughs best

El que sacó a Carrillo, perdió el banquillo - If you leave your seat, you lose your seat

El que se fue para La Barranca perdió la banca - If you leave your seat, you lose your seat

El que se mete a jugar tiene que aguantar - If you look for trouble you have to take it.

El que se muere hinchado se muere sin arrugas - If you die bloated you die without wrinkles

El que se quema con la leche hasta la cuajada sopla - If you know trouble you stay away from it

El que siembra vientos, cosecha tempestades - If you do something bad to someone, the same will happen to you

El que siembra y cria, gana de noche y gana de día - The hard worker always receives rewards

El que tenga frio que jale cobija - Solve your own problems

El que tenga rosario que lleve la cuenta - One should keep count of their own faults

El que tiene boca a Roma va - Persistence is a good quality to have

El que tiene tejado de vidrio que no tire piedras al del vecino - People who live in glass houses shouldn't throw stones

El que tiene tienda que la atienda - The one with the store has to attend it

El que toma consejo muere de viejo - Is not wise to always take advice

El que va para Limón pierde el sillón - If you lose your place in line you don't get it back

El que tiene la yegua tiene el potrillo - If you have something good, you have it all

El tiempo perdido hasta los santos lo lloran - Time should never be wasted

El tiempo vuela - Time flies

El tigre salta detrás de cualquier matón - A bully person can encounter trouble

El toro viejo, con la pechonada tiene - Old bull can only count of his broad chest (elders may count on being wise)

El trueno es presagio de la tempestad - Pay attention when warnings come your way

El vivo no dice lo que sabe y el tonto no sabe lo que dice - The clever one doesn´t say what he knows and the fool doesn´t know what he says

En arca abierta, hasta el justo peca - It's difficult to resist temptation when it stares you in the face

En bocas cerradas no entran moscas - It's better to keep one's mouth closed and be discrete

En dos toques – Immediately

En el infierno pide cobija - A person who is always cold

En esta casa mando yo cuando mi mujer no está - I am the boss in my house, when my wife isn´t there

En Heredia el que no tiene un loco en la casa se lo pide prestado al vecino: in Heredia (Costa Rica) - If they don´t have a crazy in their family, they borrow one

En la casa del sastre todo son tiras y en la del zapatero todo es mentiras: - Better to guard against appearances

En la manada siempre hay un toro rompedor - There is always a dissident in a large group

En la puerta del horno se quema el pan - Sometimes the worse things happen near home

En la variedad está el gusto - Variety is the spice of life

En las malas se conocen los amigos - Friends are well known in bad times

En los tiempos de upa, la gente usaba la jupa - In the old times there were true thinkers

En martes no te cases ni te embarques - Don't do things on Tuesday (superstition)

En paz y tratando - Said when a business deal is closed

En río revuelto, ganancia de pescadores - Some people profit from bad situations

En todo hay bueno y malo - There is bad and good in everything

En un abrir y cerrar de ojos – Instantly

En un entierro quiere ser el muerto - Wants to be the center of attention always

En una que va y otra que viene - One of these days

Encontrar la horma del zapato - To look for the thing that fits

Engañar con la vaina vacía - To preach qualities you don´t have

Entre bueyes no hay cornadas; Entre gitanos no nos sacamos el naipe - Friends take care of one another

Entre camagua y elote - Something half-done

Entre la espada y la pared - To be between a rock and a hard place

Ente más alto más dura la caída - The bigger they are the harder they fall

Entre más aspirina le dan, mas le sube la calentura; Entre más se retira el cabro más duro el guevazo - Sometimes the cure is worse than the medicine

Entre marido y mujer nadie puede meter - Don't get involved with married people's problems

Entre menos bulto más claridad - The fewer people the better

Errar es humano, y perdonar es divino - To make mistakes is human, to forgive is virtuous

Es más la bulla que el aguacero - Something that is not as important as it seems

Es mejor comer pollo a medias que mierda solo - Is better to have company than being alone

Es mejor deber dinero que no favores - Is better to owe money than to owe favors

Es mejor llegar tarde, que no llegar nunca - Better late than never

Es mejor malo conocido que bueno por conocer - It's better to stick with what you have than seek the unknown

Es mejor morir de indigestión que de hambre - Better to have indigestion that to die from hunger

Es mejor no creer en renquera de perro ni en lágrimas de mujer - Better not to believe in a lame dog or in women´s tears

Es mejor prevenir que lamentar - Better safe than sorry

Es mejor tonto callado que tonto hablando - It is better to keep your mouth closed if you don't know what you are talking about

Es mejor un buen arreglo que un mal pleito - It's better to work things out than fight

Es mejor una amistad que una tripa torcida - Better to fart in front of friends than to be gassy

Es tan flaco que parece que empeño el fondillo - A very skinny person

Es una candela muy grande para un santo tan chiquitico - The candle is bigger than the saint (someone unworthy of something)

Es una vaina - It´s a pity, a dilemma

Es una vaina ser un chollado - What a pity to be penniless!

Esas son palabras mayores - Something said of utter importance

Ese carajo es tan viejo que fue ascensorista en la torre de Babel - A very old person

Ese cuento es más viejo que la maña de pedir fiado - That´s a very old tale

Eso fue la gota que derramó el vaso - The straw that broke the camel's back

Eso fue en el año del fusil de chispa - That happened in the flint rifle times (that happened in the old times)

Esos pecados son los que el padre no pregunta - There are sins too bad to tell

Esta en cama - To be sick

Esta es la misma vaca, pero sin las patas de atrás - When things look the same to a person

Estar a manga por hombro - A messy, disorderly person

Estar acabangad; tener cabanga - To feel nostalgy, sadness

Estar ajado: To be old, used, dirty

Estar apagado - To have no enthusiasm

Estar aplanado: - To be idle

Estar aquerenciado - To have roots in a place

Estar arrejuntado - To live out of wedlock

Estar aumentada - To be pregnant

Estar cabriado - To be mad

Estar carretoneado - Used and in bad condition (can refer to people as well)

Estar catrineado - Spiffy, well-dressed

Estar como agua para chocolate - To be mad

Estar como gallo en patio ajeno - To feel out of place

Estar como jarro de loco - In bad shape, badly bruised (a car with many dents on it)

Estar como pez en agua - To be doing something you like

Estar como que si, como que no - To be indecisive

Estar como sardina en lata - To be in a crowded space

Estar como una paipa – A skinny person

Estar como un toro guaco – To be very angry

Estar como una pasa - To look old

Estar como una uva - To look well

Estar como usted cuando era pobre - A humorous answer when some greets you

Estar con agua al cuello - To be in a jam

Estar con el indio arriba - To be in a bad mood

Estar con el moco caído - To be depressed

Estar con la paja tras la oreja - to have doubts about something, somebody

Estar con el rabo entre las patas - To be like a chastised dog (with the tail between the legs)

Estar con el rancho ardiendo - To be pregnant

Estar con la cabeza gacha - To be humiliated

Estar con la panza pegada al espinazo - Hungry

Estar con las llaves perdidas - To have the runs

Estar con permiso del panteonero - To be living on borrowed time

Estar con salidera - To have diahrea

Estar con una pata adentro y otra afuera - To be indecisive

Estar con una pata en el cementerio - To be gravelly ill

Estar con una pata en el estribo - One foot aboard the plane or ready to go somewhere

Estar chiva - To be mad

Estar chonete - To be without money

Estar de a tiro - To be in good shape

Estar de Daguves a Libera - Out of work

Estar de brazos cruzados - Not do anything

Estar de buenas - To be in a good mood or lucky

Estar de cabanga - To be sad

Estar de chicha - To be in a bad mood

Estar de luna; Estar de mal café - To be in a bad mood

Estar de manteles largos - To be partying

Estar de mediodía para abajo - To be older than

Estar de rajar con la uña - To be in good health

Estar detrás del palo - To be totally unaware of something

Estar en alas de cucaracha - To be in danger

Estar en camagua y elote - To not finish something

Estar en dime que te diré - To be a gossip

Estar en el tamal - To be well aware of things

Estar en horas extra - To be old

Estar en la danza - To be involved in a dirty business

Estar en la lista negra - To be on the black list

Estar en la lona - To be poor

Estar en la luna - Distracted or absent minded

Estar en las últimas - To be near death

Estar en pañales - Lacking experience

Estar en la pura tusa - To be penniless

Estar en su charco - To do what one likes

Estar encuetado - To be furious

Estar entre la espada y la pared - To be over a barrel

Estar entreverado - Green coffee grains among ripe ones

Estar esgonzado - Loose like a marionette

Estar estorrentado - To know nothing of his/hers whereabouts

Estar fiambre - Stale food

Estar fuera del guacal: an opinion without good bases

Estar hasta el copete - Fed up with something or someone

Estar hasta el pescuezo - To be fed up with something

Estar hasta la cara me duele - To be totally drunk

Estar hasta la cincha; Estar hasta las hachas - To be totally drunk

Estar hasta la mecha - To be drunk

Estar hasta las telarañas - To be in love

Estar hecho leña - To be broke, sick

Estar hecho un puño - Top be afraid

Estar joco - Something spoiled

Estar mal del techo - To be crazy

Estar más de mediodía para abajo; Estoy como maduro en bajo - Something difficult
    to attain

Estar más enredado que el nudo del diablo - To be difficult

Estar más jalado que un mecate de campanario - An emaciated person

Estar más limpio que tabla de dulce - To be without money

Está mas pelao que la tabla de raspar dulce - To be penniless

Estar mírame y no me toques - A touchy person

Estar mordisqueado - Something with a bite in it

Estar por las nubes – Expensive

Estar puestitico - To be interested in someone else

Estar que se lo lleva los diablos - Mad

Estar quemado - Out of style or in disuse

Estar sin pinol - To be without money

Estar sin un cinco - Broke

Estar sobre la jugada - To be on top of things or business

Estar tablas - To be even (not owe money)

Estar todo patas arriba - Sloppy

Estar una cosa sobre el tapete - To be discussing or debating something

F

Falta el rabo por desollar - There is still work to do, to finish
Faltarle a uno un tornillo - To be missing a screw or crazy
Favor con favor se paga - Favor with favor gets paid

G

Gallina vieja hace buen caldo - Old women have their attributes
Gallo viejo con el ala mata - Experience is what counts
Gastar pólvora en zopilotes - To waste something
Gastar saliva - To waste time talking
Gato maullador no es buen cazador - Tooting your horn doesn´t make you good
Genio y figura hasta la sepultura - Some people never change
Gorrearse a alguien - To bully someone

H

Hablando se entiende la gente - When there is communication, there is
    understanding
Hablar como lora hambrienta - To talk a lot
Hablar con plata Blanca - To speak honestlty and frankly
Hablar es plata, callar es oro - There is more reward in silence than in
    conversation
Hablar hasta por los codos - To talk a lot
Hablar más que un heredero inconforme ; Hablar hasta por el hueso de la nuca - A very
    talkative person
Hablar menos, hacer más - Talk less, do more
Hablar yeguadas - To say stupid things
Hablarle hasta un muerto - A gutsy person, without fear to face something
Hacer agua la boca - To cause envy

Hacer buchaca - To save money

Hacer chanchadas - To do bad things

Hacer chanchullo - To commit fraud

Hacer de tripas, chorizo - To make a big effort

Hacer el bien no cuesta nada - To do good is easy

Hacer una diligencia; ir a matar un venado; ir a cortar flores; me está llamando el rey -
    Having to go quickly to the bathroom for number 2

Hacer el encargo - To get pregnant

Hacer el quite - To dodge

Hacer leña del árbol caído - To take advantage of a person who is down and out

Hacer números - To figure something out

Hacer ojitos - Make eyes at someone or flirt

Hacer por pura chepa - To guess something accidentally

Hacer serio - To stare someone down

Hacer su agosto - To do a business deal

Hacer trompas - To get mad

Hacer un camarón - To do a small job

Hacer una raya en el cielo - To do something short of a miracle

Hacer una torta - To get in a jam or do something stupid

Hacer una vaca - To pass the hat to collect money

Hacer ver chinos con sombrillas - To see stars

Hacer viejitas - To skip stones over water

Hacerle a uno la cama - To pull the rug out from under someone

Hacerle la cruz - To ignore someone we dislike

Hacernos la boca agua - To envy

Hacerse el chanco - To play dumb

Hacerse el loco - To ignore something

Hacerse el muerto pa´ que lo carguen - To pretend to be in trouble to get help

Hacerse leña - To destroy something

Hacerse un chorro de humo - To disappear

Hacerse un nudo - To be in a knot

Hay gente para todo - Some people will do anything

Hasta tirar pa´rriba - To have something in abundance

Hay más tiempo que vida - Don't worry about everyday problems

Hay moros en la costa - There is danger lurking

Hay mucha tela que cortar - A lot of unfinished business

Hay mucho paño para cortar y el saco está lleno - There is more than meets the eye

Hay que comprar cuando venden y vender cuando compran - Learn to take advantage of your opportunities

Hay que hacerse el chancho pa comerse al tigre - You got to pretend not to understand sometimes to be on top

Hay que joder al amigo porque el enemigo no se déjà - Taking advantage of a friend when the enemy is not around

Hay que pegar duro pero con guante de seda - Hit hard but wear a silk glove

Hay que quitarse el sombrero - Take your hat off to someone or admire them

Hay que saberle buscar la comba al palo - Look for the right side of things

Hay que ser lagarto y gallo, tener colmillo y espuela - To approach things with tooth and nail.

Hay que tener más miedo al rayo que a la raya - Something bad can happen anytime

Hay quienes se les da la mano y se agarran hasta el codo - There are people who like to take advantage of everything

Hay un gato encerrado - There is more than meets the eye

Haz bien y no mirar a quien - Do good deeds for nothing in return

Hecha la ley, hecha la trampa - There are laws with loops

Hierba mala nunca muere - It's hard for a bad person to change

Hijo de tigre sale pintado - Like father like son. Chip off the old block

Hombre casado, papel quemado - Beware of married men

Hombre pendejo no goza de mujer bonita - A coward man is not admired by pretty women

Hombre prevenido nunca fue vencido - A well prepared man is never defeated

Hombre prevenido vale por dos - A well prepared person is worth the same as two people

Hoy por ti, mañana por mí - One good turn deserves another

Hoy somos mañana no somos - Luck can change

Huir del fuego y caer de las brasas - To end up in worse place than where started from

I

Indio comido, puesto al camino - To eat and run

Indio que canta es porque quiere huir - When you get a message, pay attention to it

Indio sentado quiere otro bocado - Idle person wants to be helped

Ir a dar misa a otra parte - To tell someone to go to hell

Ir a escorar- To end up in another place, a different location

Ir al caite, ir en el carro de don Fernando - To go somewhere on foot

Ir al grano - To get to the point

Ir al paso de la guayaba - To move slowly or fall behind

Ir al serrucho - To go fifty/fifty or split the cost

Ir come entierro de pobre - To move or go fast

Ir con la música a otra parte - Take your business somewhere else

Ir cuesta abajo - To go downhill (figurative)

Ir para tras como el cangrejo - To go backwards like a crab

Ir por lana y salir trasquilada - A deal that didn´t work as expected

Ir que le vuela la bata; va que le vuela la chaqueta - To pass by in a big hurry

Irse al carajo - To tell someone to go to hell

Irse con la música a otra parte - To tell someone to go to hell

Irse donde calienta mejor el sol - To go where it suits you best

Irse el alma a los talones - To have a big scare

Irsele arriba el apellido - A person with a very short fuse

Irse lo comido por lo servido - Difficult tomake ends meet

Irse por la tangente - To go off on a tangent

Írsele a uno el apellido - To get mad

Írsele a uno la mano - To get carried away with something

Írsele a uno la pajarita - To forget

Írsele el pajarito - To forget something

Írsele por mal camino - Go down the wrong tube (choke on food)

J

Jalar el hule - To fall in love

Jalan más un par de tetas que un tractor; Jalan mas dos tetas que cien carretas - Two female teets (breasts) can pull harder

Jala más un piojo en alquitrán - A louse stuck in petroleum can pull harder (someone with little strength to pull

Jalarle las orejas a San Jorge - To play darts

Jalarse una parada - To make a serious mistake

Jalarse una torta - To make someone pregnant

Juege con el santo menos con la limosna - Don´t play with the sacred

Juego de mano se queda para los villanos - Hand games attract bad company

Jugar con fuego - To play with fire (figurative)

Jugar sucio - To betray someone or play dirty

Jugarse el pellejo - To risk ones hide

Jugársela entera - To risk it all

Juntarse el hambre con las ganas de comer - People who share similar traits, skills

Juntate con los buenos y serás uno de ellos - You are as good as your friends

Juntos pero no revueltos - Together but not involved romantically

L

La belleza sin gracia es una flor que no huele - Beauty without grace is no beauty at all

La cabra siempre tira al monte - Everyone acts according to their own nature

La cara es el espejo del alma - The face is the mirror of the soul

La caridad empieza por la casa - Charity begins at home

La cáscara guarda el palo - Phrase used for people don´t like to bathe

La chiquita que es llorona y la madre que la pellizca - Someone who is easily swayed into doing anything

La codicia rompe el saco - It´s not good to crave other people´s riches

La cuchara sabe lo que necesita la olla - Friends know their friends´troubles

La diligencia es permitida: - To be diligent is always preferred

La dicha de la fea, la bonita la desea - Sometimes unattractive women are happier in marriage than beautiful women

La dicha de la fea a la bonita le importa un pito - The luck of the ugly is not mind by the pretty

La esencia no viene en barriles - Good things come in small packages

La esencia no viene en estañones - Big things come in small packages

La esencia viene en frascos pequeños - Fine essence come in small jars

La esperanza el lo último que se pierde - Don't lose hope

La fe mueve montañas - Faith moves mountains

La gallina vieja es la que le da sabor al caldo - A worthy thing, makes things worthy

La gracia del sapo no está en el brinco - Some people have hidden abilities

La gracia no estar en orinar sino en hacer espuma - It is not important to do something, but how to do it

La jarana sale a la cara - Debtors are easy to tell apart

La letra con sangre entra - Practice makes perfect

La manta encoge o estira - Old cotton shrinks or gives (things adjust to circumstances)

La mejor palabra es la que no se habla; En boca cerrada no entra mosca - A discrete person always knows when not to talk

La miel no se hizo para zopilotes - People who do not appreciate good things, do not deserve them

La mosca busca la miel y el bolsillo de los hombres quien lo busca es la mujer - Flies are attracted to honey, and women to men´s pocket

La necesidad tiene cara de caballo - People will do anything for money if they really need it

La pereza es mala consejera - Laziness is bad

La piedra que está en el fondo no sabe lo que el sol calienta - If it is not your problem, you don´t little about it

La plata jala plata - Money makes more money

La pobreza no es deshonra - Being poor is not a shame

La práctica hace al maestro - Practice makes perfect

La primer impresión es lo que vale - The first impression is the one that counts

La procesión va por dentro - To keep your problems bottled up

La risa abunda en la boca de los tontos - To laugh all the time can be seen as foolish

La ropa sucia se lava en casa - Keep your dirty laundry at home

La sangre jala - Blood is thicker than water

La suerte de la fea, la rica la desea - Unattractive women have better luck on marriage than beautiful women

La suegra como la yuca, más enterrada mejor - Mother-in-law, is better far away

La unión hace la fuerza - Solidarity is important

La verdad es para decirla, no para ocultarla - The truth is to be told, not hidden

La verdad no peca pero incomoda - The truth hurts

La vida es dura, después viene la muerte - Life is hard, then comes death

La vida es para vivirla - Life is to be lived

Ladrón que roba a ladrón cien años de perdón - It's all right to do something bad against a bad person

Lágrimas de cocodrilo - Fake tears

Las apariencias engañan - Looks are deceiving

Las cosas caen por su peso - Things fall by their own weight

Las cosas no son del dueño sino del que las necesita - Things are of the ones who need them

Las cosas son del cristal con que se pueden ver - Things are seem through the glass one looks at it

Las cosas se toman de quien vienen - Things are taken for that they are worth

Las desgracias nunca vienen solas - Difficulties rarely come alone

Las mejores cargas siempre caminan atrás - Valuable cargo usually go in the back (it is not always best to take the lead)

Las palabras hablan, los escritos quedan - Putting something in writing is better than to just talk

Las paredes oyen - The walls have ears

Las pavas tirándole a las escopetas - The disciples teaching the master

Las tristezas de hoy, alegrías del mañana - sadness today, happiness tomorrow

Lavarse las manos - Wash hands of a responsibility

Levantarse con el pie derecho - To get up with the right foot

Levantarse con el pie izquierdo - To get up with the left foot

Lo barato sale caro - You get what you pay for

Lo mismo es Chana que Juana - Equals to the same thing

Lo que abunda no daña - Live off the fat of the land

Lo que abunda no estorba - Abundance doesn´t get in the way

Lo que bien se aprende no se olvida - You won't forget what you learn well

Lo que conviene, viene - What has to happen, happens

Lo que el doctor yerra se tapa con tierra - Doctor´s mistakes get buried with earth

Lo que empieza mal, mal termina - What starts badly, finishes badly

Lo que es bueno para el ganso es bueno para la gansa - What's good for the goose is good for the gander

Lo que fue en mi año, no fue en mi daño - Excesses not always hurt

Lo que mal empieza mal termina - What begins bad ends bad

Lo que no mata engorda - If it doens´t kill you, it will fatten you up

Lo que no nos cuesta, hagámoslo fiesta - Don't appreciate things you don't have to work hard to obtain

Lo que no se mueve se hace pelota - What it doesn´t move, it hardens

Lo que no tiene dinga tiene mandinga - Not everything is perfect

Lo que por agua viene por agua se va - Easy come, easy go

Lo que se da y se quita, se vuelve cuita - Don´t ask back for what you have given away

Lo que se hace con la mano lo borra el codo - A bad action cancels out a good one

Lo que se hereda no se hurta - What´s inherited is not stolen

Lo que tiene que suceder sucede - What has to happen, happens

Los buenos amigos se conocen cuando se está en la cama o en la cárcel - Good friends are known you when you get in trouble

Los lunes ni las gallinas ponen - Nobody wants to work on Monday after a weekend of partying

Los molinos de Dios muelen despacio pero muy finito - People´s good actions will be rewarded at the end

Los niños y los borrachos siempre dicen la verdad - Children and drunks always say the truth

Los vivos viven de los tontos y los tontos de trabajar - Clever people live from fools and the fools from working hard (sometimes people like to take advantage of others)

LL

Llegar a la hora del burro - To arrive late
Llegar a la raíz del cacho - To get to the bottom of something
Llenarse la cabeza de humo - To become arrogant
Llenársele a uno la cachimba - To have ones patience wears out
Llevar la batuta - To be in command
Llevar palo - To suffer the consequences of something
Llevarla suave - To take things calmly
Llevarse al carajo - Also to spoil or ruin something
Llevarse candanga - To get into big trouble
Llover sobre mojado - To repeat the same mistake

M

Machete, estáte en tu vaina - Watch out!, think what you are doing
Majar el rabo - To humiliate
Majar los talones - To follow someone closely
Mal de muchos, consuelo de tontos - A common difficulty is a difficulty shared by many
Mal de uno bien de otro - Bad things to some, can be good things to others
Mamar la lengua - To speak exactly like another person
¡Manda guevo! - An action that is hard to understand
Mandar al otro lado - To kill
Mañana oscura, tarde segura - Bad weather in the morning, good weather in the afternoon
Martes ni te cases ni te embarques - Tuesdays are unlucky days
Más abajo pisó Colón - An expression used when someone steps on you
Más aburrido que un chancho en una alforja - As bored as a pig in a sac (someone/something very bored)
Más agarrado que mono en ventolero - A tight fisted person
Más agarrado que una viejita en moto - A tight fisted person

Más agüevado que perico en taro - As bored as a parekeet in a can (someone/ something very bored)

Más cerrado que un bombillo - To not understand anything

Más caliente que un jarro sonto - Hotter than a mug without the handle

Más contento que novia en víspera de matrimonio - Very happy

Más delicado que una cría de chompipes - A touchy person

Más difícil que sacarle caldo a un riel - To be difficult

Más difícil que sacarle un pedo a un muñeco - To be difficult (vulgar)

Más enredado que el nudo del Diablo - As tangled as the devil´s knot (someone very complicated)

Más feo que un carro por debajo - To be ugly

Más feo que el golpe de espinilla - Pain is hard to take

Más feo que ver morir a la madre - To be ugly

Más incómodo que dormir con la suegra – More uncomfortable than sleeping with your mother-in-law

Más incómodo que una piedra en un zapato - As bothersome as a rock in a shoe

Más lerdo que la quijada de arriba - Slower than the upper jaw (a person who moves slowly)

Más jugado que el doble cero - A person who has had a lot of sexual or life experience

Más jugado que un vikingo - A person who has had a lot of sexual or life experience

Más largo que un domingo sin plata - Boring or something that seems to last forever

Más largo que un pedo de culebra - To be very long (vulgar)

Más largo que un silbido de lechero - Longer than the milkman´s whistle (a tall, skinny man)

Más largo que una meada en moto - To be very long (vulgar)

Más limpio que cuello de monja - To have no money

Más limpio que chaqueta de salonero - To have no money

Más limpio que el fustán de María Santísima - Someone/something very clean

Más limpio que la tabla del dulce - Financially struggling

Más metido que un yuyo - As enroached as athetle foot: someone hard to get rid of

Más nerviosa que recién casada - More nervous than a newlywed

Más pegado que una garrapata - Someone who is your shadow and is always with you

Más perdido que Tarzan el día de la madre - To be lost of off track

Más perdido que un pedo en un baile - To be lost or off track

Más perdido que un perro en misa - To be lost or off track

Más pesado que cargar un elefante - An obnoxious person

Más sabe el diablo por viejo que por diablo - Experience is what counts

Más salado que moco de marinero - Unlucky

Más sencillo que un calzoncillo de manta - Humbler than old cotton underwear (a very humble person)

Más serio que burro en lancha - To be serious

Más serio que mono con banano de plástico - To be very serious

Más serio que un cinco de ques; Más serio que un burro cruzando un río - A very serious person

Más soplado que entierro de pobre - To be fast

Más tieso que cocodrilo enyesado - As rigid as a crocodile in a cast (someone/something very stiff)

Más tieso que un pan de tres días - As rigid as a crocodile in a cast (someone/something very stiff)

Más triste que un domingo sin plata - To be sad

Más tocada que pila de agua bendita - To be touched as much as blessed water

Más vale maña que fuerza - Intelligence is better than brute force

Más vale pájaro en la mano que cien volando - A bird in the hand is worth two in the bush

Más vale pan con amor que gallina con dolor - Is better poverty with love, than wealth with pain

Más vale poco y bueno que mucho y malo -A little good is better than a lot of bad

Más vale prevenir que lamentar - Better safe than sorry

Más vale que digan □ aquí corrió□ que aquí murió□ : - Is better to say "he ran, than he died"

Más vale reir que llorar - Is better to laugh than to cry

Más vale sabio callado que tonto hablando: better a wise person silent than a fool speaking

Más vale ser cabeza de ratón que cola de león - A big fish in a little pond

Más vale ser que parecer: it is better to be than to appear to be

Más vale que sobre y no que falte - It is better to have too much than too little

Más vale solo que mal acompañado - It's better to be alone than in bad company

Más vale tarde que nunca - Better late than ever

Más vale una amistad perdida que una tripa torcida - Said after one passes gas in public

Más viejo que la sarna - A very old person

Matar dos pájaros de una sola piedra - Kill two birds with one stone

Matar la culebra - To be lazy

Me cayeron las siete plagas de Egipto - To have all the illnesses in the world

¡Me extraña araña! - To be surprised

Me salió más caro el caldo que los huevos - Something that ended up worse that it started out

Mejor caerse que andar guindando - It is better to fall that to keep hanging

Mejor convencer que vencer - It is better to convince than to win in a fight

Mejor machete, estáte en tu vaina - Is better to keep out of trouble

Mejor por bien que por mal - It is better to do things the right way than the wrong way

Mejor ser deseado que no sobrado - It is better to be desired than to be ignored

Menear tablas - To dance

Menos indios más guineas - Less people, more of everything

Mentar la soga en casa del ahorcado - To say something in bad taste

Mentarle a uno la madre - To insult

Meter a la chirola - To put in jail

Meter el gol - To deceive

Meter en la chirola - To jail someone

Meter la cuchara - To butt into a conversation or interrupt

Meter la mano en el fuego por alguien - To defend someone

Meter la mano en la pila de agua bendita - To do something that is not allowed

Meter la mano por alguien - To help someone

Meter las narices - To be nosy or snoopy

Meter polla por gallina - To trick someone into thinking they are getting something good

Meterá uno una jáquima - To swindle someone

Meterse en un berenjenal - To get into difficult trouble

Metersele el agua - To be moody

Meterse en boca del lobo - To be in a dangerous situation

Meterse en la camisa de once varas - To get into something over one's head

Meterse en un colocho - To get into a jam

Mi gozo en un pozo - My happiness is without limits

Miar fuera del taro - To give a wrong opinion about something

Mientras el cuerpo aguante, adelante - While the body takes it, go for it

Mientras más trepa el mono más enseña el culo - Fast climbers exposed their rear ends faster

Montársele a uno - To bother a person

Mover cielo y tierra - To make a big effort

Mover el esqueleto - To dance

Mucha música y nada de ópera - All talk and no action

Mucho ruido, pocas nueces - That much noise for nothing

Mujer, tórtola y gato, a cual más de los tres ingratos - Woman, love bird and cat, all of them equally ungrateful

Mujer y lora hablan mucho y dicen poco - Woman and parrot talk a lot but say little

Músico pagado no toca buen son: Don't pay someone in advance; it is better to pay for something at the end, and not at the beginning

N

Nacer parado - To have good luck

Nació con las patas hinchadas - Born with swollen feet (downtrotten)

Nadie es billete de mil pesos pa 'gustarle a todo el mundo - Nobody is a dollar bill to be liked by everyone

Nadie es profeta en su propia tierra - No one is prophet in their own land

Nadie escarmienta en cabeza ajena - One can only learn by own experience

Nadie le pone la pata - No one is as good as him/her

Nadie me maja el rabo - It is difficult to find faults on that person

Nadie nace aprendido - Practice makes perfect

Nadie se muere en la víspera - Don't worry about things too much

Nadie sirve bien a dos amos - Nobody serve two masters well at the same time

Ni a balas – No way!

Ni a palos - No way!

Ni loco - No way!

Ni lerdo ni perezoso - Quick to take action

Ni más ni menos - Just the right amount

Ni papa - Nothing

Ni para la masa para el perico - Not enough of something

Ni pica leña ni presta hacha - Used for egotistical people

Ni raja leña ni presta el hacha - More of an obstacle than help

Ni tan cerca que queme el santo, ni tan lejos que no lo alumbre - It is good to have a middle ground on most things

Ningún lagarto tiene boca grande hasta que tenes que cruzar el río - It is not until you have to face it, than the problem really begins

Ningún mono ve su rabo - It's hard for people to see their own defects

Ningún panadero dice que su pan es malo - No one believes what they do is bad

No aguantar carga - To have a short fuse, to be intolerant

No alcanza ni el cábuz - A person who never marries

No andar con piquetes - Don't beat around the bush

No apearse ni en las cuestas. - A man who constantly makes his wife pregnant

No arranca pelo sin sangre -People who won't do things unless they get something in return

No asolearse ni menos serenarse - Not wanting to take part of something

No bailo ni los ojos - To not know how to dance

No bailo ni trompo - To not know how to dance

No busques tres patas al gato - Don't look for trouble

No cabecear ni en un rezo - A soccer term. a soccer term (does not know how throw the ball with the head)

No comer cuento - A person who cannot be deceived

No componer nada - Is not good for nothing

No confiarle a uno ni un saco de alacranes - To not trust anyone

No confundir la gordura con el hinchazón - Don't confuse things

No conocer en donde está el queso - To be ignorant about something

No creer que porque el perro lleva el hocico estirado, es porque va silbando - Things are not always what they appear to be

No cuente los pollos antes de que nazcan - Don't count your chickens before they hatch

No dar a brazo a torcer - To not yield

No dar ni frío ni calor - To be indifferent

No dar sal para un huevo - To be tight

No decir ni tus ni mus; Sin decir tusa ni musa - To say nothing good or bad about something

No dejes par mañana lo que puedes hacer hoy - Don't leave for tomorrow what you can do today

No digas que llueve, hasta que truene - Don´t stay someone until you have proof of it

No echar más leña a la hoguera - Don´t make things worse by rehashing the same things

No es cierto que todo tiempo pasado fue major - Not true that the past was better than the present

No es lo mismo jodido que estar jodiendo - It is not the same to be unlucky than to be annoying

No es ni chicha ni limonada - To be indifferent about something

No es tan chancho! - He is not that bad!

No es tan fiero el león como lo pintan - He is not as fiercy as they say

No están todos los que son, ni son todos los que están - Not everyone that should be here, is here

No ha parido la vaca y ya está mamando el ternero - When someone does something in a big hurry

No hace falta el que se va sino el que se viene - When someone leaves and won´t be missed

No hay como el zapato viejo - Something old is better than something new

No hay corazón traidor a su dueño - The heart is never a traitor

No hay enemigo pequeño - There is no small enemy

No hay grupera que no chime - All jobs and businesses present problems

No hay mal por bien no venga - It's not meant to be

No hay más carga pesada que una mala conciencia - A bad conscious is the heaviest weight

No hay más que arar con los buecitos que tenemos - We have to do with what we have

No hay más tren que el que pita - Train, only the one with a whistle

No hay mejor salsa que el hambre - Hunger is the best spice

No hay nada peor que vivir arrimado - There is nothing worse than to beg for a place to stay

No hay novia fea ni muerto malo - There are no ugly sweethearts or bad dead people

No hay peor negocio que ser mala yegua - It is bad business to deal with bullies

No hay panza sin ombligo - Almost anything can be difficult

No hay peor cuña que la del mismo palo - There is no worse enemy than someone who has been very close to us like a friend or family

No hay peor sordo que el que no quiere oír - There is no worse deaf person than one who doesn't want to listen

No hay peor tonto que el que no quiere aprender - There is no worse fool than the one who doesn´t want to learn

No hay tres que tengan el guaro de igual manera - Booze has a different effect on different people

No hay que brincar estando el suelo parejo - Don't make waves if things are well

No hay que confundir la gordura con el hinchazón - Don't judge things by their appearance

No hay que contar la plata delante de los pobres: it is better not to flaunt things in front of others

No hay que creer en santos que orinan - Not to believe in miracles

No hay que creer ni dejar de creer - Is good to believe but is also good to doubt

No hay que creer que porque el cangrejo está en la playa es porque es turista; no hay que creer que porque el perro levanta la pata es porque es karateca - Appearances can be misleading

No hay que darle la espalda al toro: It is better to be cautious with bullies

No hay que deberle al rico ni ofrecerle al pobre - Better to owe nothing to the poor or to the wealthy

No hay que desconfiar de caballo flaco - Don't be fooled by appearances

No hay que echarle perlas a los chanchos - Don´t waste your riches on pigs

No hay que gastar pólvora en zopilotes - Don´t waste your energies with the unworthy

No hay que jalarle mucho el rabo a la ternera - Everything has its limits

No hay que llegar primero, pero hay que saber llegar - To be first is not as important as to get there

No hay que mezclar el aceite con la manteca - Don´t try mixing the oil with the lard (don´t confuse apples with oranges)

No hay que pasarse de bueno - To be too nice is not always good

No hay que poner toda la carne en el asador - It is better to hold onto somethings instead of nothing

No hay que ser tirado con los pobres ni rebajado con los ricos - Better not to be arrogant with the poor or feel diminished with the wealthy

No hay reglas sin excepción - There is always an exception to the rule

No hay tal culebra de pelo - No such thing

No hay tu tía - There is no way to solve the problem

No limpiarle a uno ni los zapatos - To be inferior to someone

No matar ni una mosca - Someone who appears prude

No me la hace bueno - Something is fishy here!

No mires para afuera sin mirar para adentro - One should look at his own defects

No pegar el ojo - Not be able to sleep

No perder patada - To always be on target

No perdonar pelo, color, ni tamaño - Someone who is very demanding all the time

No poder tocar ni con un palo - Won't touch something not even with a ten foot pole

No poder ver a un pobre acomodado - To envy someone

No ponga el sombrero donde no lo pueda alcanzar - Your goals should be always managable

No por mucho madrugar amanece más temprano - Things happen at the right time

No pueden los vivos y van a poder los muertos - Things not accomplished by the clever, can hardly get accomplished by fools

No puede ver caballo porque le ofrece viaje - Someone who likes to take advantage of others

No pueden ver un pobre acomodado - Some people are bothered by the idleness of others

No quebrar ni un plato - Someone very timid

No quedar otro palo en que ahorcarse - Try to adjust to the circusntances

No rueda porque le estorban los brazos - Someone so fat that can roll

No se mienta la soga en la casa del ahorcado - It is better to be discrete at difficult times

No se puede cagar para arriba - It is better to be humble than arrogant

No se puede quedar bien con todos - You can not be liked by everyone

No saber ni donde está parado - A person who has no knowledge of something

No sacar ni una vaca del fondo - An inefficient lawyer, person

No se afloje ni se aflija - Don´t get sad or give up

No se coma la vaca antes de matarla; No se puede amansar el potro antes que haya parido la yegua - All things should be done at their due time

No ser comida de trompudo - To be difficult

No ser cosa del otro mundo - To be no big deal

No ser chicha ni limonada - To be wishy-washy

No servir ni para trapo de comal: To be a nobody

No siempre el mejor camino es el más corto - The shortest route is not always the best one

No somos muchos pero somos machos - We are not many but we are courageous

No solo de pan vive el hombre: - Man does not live of bread alone

No soltar el churuco - To not let others talk

No tener arte ni parte - It is none of your business

No tener cama en que caer muerto - To be very poor

No tener cerebro ni para un derrame - To be stupid

No tener pelos en la lengua - Not afraid to speak one's mind

No tener perro que me ladre - Someone very independent

No tener un pelo de tonto - To be very intelligent

No tener una cosa ni pies ni cabeza - Not to be able to make heads or tales of something

No tener vela en este entierro - You have no part on this!

No tire piedras quien tenga techo de vidrio - It is better not to critical when having faults of your own

No todo el monte es orégano - Life isn't a rose garden

No todo lo que brilla es oro - All that glitters is not gold

No todo lo que roncan es tigre - Things aren´t always what they appear

No tragarse el anzuelo - Not to swallow the bate (figurative)

No valer ni un cinco - To be penniless

No vale un papirotazo en las narices - It´s not worth the effort

Nunca digas de esta agua no beberé - Don´t ever say never

Nunca falta un remendado para un descosido - There is always someone for someone else

Nunca es tarde para empezar - It is never too late to begin

Nunca es tarde si la dicha es buena - The wait is worth while

Nunca falta un borracho en una vela - There is always a jerk in a crowd

Nunca falta un roto para un descosido - To be made for each other

Nunca falta una olla que remendar - There are always problems to solve

Nunca segundas partes fueron buenas - Second parts were never good

Nunca te dejes llevar por las primeras buenas - Don´t be lead by breaking new

O

Obras son amores y no buenas razones - Good actions are better when demostrated

Ocurrir cada muerte de obispo - Something the rarely occurs

Ofrecer cielo y tierra - To offer a lot to someone

Ofrecer el oro y el moro - Also to offer a lot to someone

Ojo al Cristo y mano a la bolsa - Be careful you don't get robbed

Ojo por ojo, diente por diente - An eye for an eye and a tooth for a tooth

Ojos que no ven corazón que no siente - What you don't know won't hurt you

Otro gallo le cantará - Better luck next time

Otro se come el cas y a mí se me hace agua la boca - When things done by others, affect you

P

Paciencia piojo que la noche es larga; hay más tiempo que vida - There is more time than life

Pagar con la misma moneda - Give someone a dose of their own medicine

Pagar el pato - To pay for something you didn´t do

Pagar el plato a medias - To pay only half for something

Pagar justos por pecadores - Sometimes people get punished for the bad deeds of others

Pagar los elotes - To suffer the consequences

Pagar los platos rotos - Suffer the consequences of something without being the one who did it

Palabras de domingo: fancy words

Pan con pan, comida de tontos - Fools think that the same thing is always good

Panza llena, corazón contento - To have eaten well

Papelitos hablan - Little papers talk

Para estar en la luna no es necesario ser astronauta - Someone who appears to be on the moon

Para la buena hambre no hay mal pan - Beggars can't be choosers

Para que darle un peine a un calvo - Don´t waste time on unworthy things

Papelitos hablan - Little papers talk

Para muestra un botón - The proof is in the sample

Para que la cuña apriete tiene que ser del mismo palo - There is no worse enemy than someone who has been very close to us like a friend or family

Para todo hay remedio, menos para la muerte - Everything has a solution

Para tonto no hay que estudiar - Said to people who commit stupid acts

Para uno que madruga, otro que no se acuesta - Better to be on the alert!

Parar la manta - To run

Parar la oreja - Listen to a conversation

Parar la tanda - To end a drunken spree

Parar la vista - To die

Parar las patas - To trip over and fall

Pararse en la escoba - To obstaculize your own project

Parársele a uno un zopilote - To be inactive

Parece que tiene hormigas en el fondillo - Ants in your pants

Parece un barril sin fondo - A big eater, never satisfied

Parece un camaleón - Someone who changes mood quickly

Parece un ropero de tres cuerpos - A fat person

Parece una merienda de negros - Said when there is a lot of noise

Parecer acordeón - To have a lot of wrinkles

Parientes y chunches viejos mejor tenerlos de lejos - Don´t be too fond of old junk

Pasar a mejor vida - To die

Pasar la brocha - To stroke or praise someone

Pasar la pelota - To "Pass the buck"

Pasar por esos aros - To share common experiences

Pasar por inocente - The equivalent of saying, "April fools"

Pasar por inocente comiendo pan callente - A joke played on someone similar to April´s Fool

Pasarse la vida rascándose la panza - Someone who likes to be idle

Pasearse el alma por el cuerpo - Someone who doesn´t worry too much

Pasearse en la olla de leche - To spoil a good project, to make a serious mistake

Paso por la escuela pero la escuela no paso por él - Someone with lots of schooling but limited manners

Patear el balde - To kick the bucket (die)

Pedir consejo a la almohada - To sleep on it (Think something over)

Pegar el gordo - To win the lottery

Pegar el grito - To protest

Pegar el ojo - To sleep

Pegar un jaretazo - When a poor person marries a rich person

Pegarse a la teta - To take advantage of something

Pegarse el gordo - To win the lottery

Pegarse la juma - To get drunk

Pegársele las cobijas - To sleep late

Peinar la culebra - To loaf or waste time

Pelar el diente - To smile

Pelar la pava - To flirt

Pelarse el rabo - To commit a mistake

Pelo de gato - Drizzle

Penas contadas son aliviadas - Sorrows shared are sorrows lessen

Peores nalgas tenia mi agüela; Peores las tenia mi suegra - It could have been worse

Perder el hilo - To forget

Perder hacha, calabaza y miel - To lose everything

Perder hasta el modo de caminar - Also to lose everything

Perder hasta las casas santas - To loose everything

Perder los bartolos - To lose your marbles

Pero nunca falta un pero - There is always an excuse for everything

Perro menos, torta más - The more the better

Perro que come huevos ni quemándole el hocico - Can't teach old dog new tricks

Perro que ladra no muerde - Someone's bark is worse than their bite

Perro sentado no caza venado - If you don´t work, you won´t eat

Perro viejo ladra echado - Old dogs barks lying down (Experience is everything)

Perro viejo ladra sentado - Experience is everything

Picarle a uno la tripa - To be hungry

Piedra que esta pa´l perro ni metiéndose en el cafetal - When things are destined for you, there is no good hiding

Piedra que rueda no cría mojo - A rolling stone gathers no moss

Piedra que rueda no echa lana - Also a rolling stone gathers no moss

Planchar la oreja - To sleep

Plata en mano, culo en cama - Pay first before making a deal

Plata en mano, culo en tierra - Pay first before making a deal

Poner abajo - To put someone down

Poner a alguien de patitas en la calle - To evict someone from their home

Poner de vuelta y media - To seduce

Poner la jupa a trabajar - To think or use head

Poner la olla al fuego - To solve a problema right away

Poner puerta afuera - To fire someone unfairly

Poner punto final - To finish something

Ponerle los puños donde la mama le puso el pezón - To hit someone on the face

Ponerse una flor en el ojal - To do something really well

Ponerse águila - To be alert or get wise

Ponerse avispa - To be alert

Ponerse bozal en el hocico - To shut up

Ponerse como chira - To blush

Ponerse como papel - To get scared

Ponerse como toro guaco - To get mad

Ponerse las botas - To become rich

Ponerse las pilas - To get wise or be alert

Ponerse un bozal en el hocico - To keep silent

Ponerse un candado en la boca - To keep quiet

Ponerse una flor en el ojal - To be successful

Ponerse vivo - To be alert or get wise

Por el vocabulario se conoce la señorita - Young ladies are known for how they talk

Poquito es bendito - A little is better than nothing

Por güevos o por candelas - To be forced to do something

Por la víspera se saca el día - You can tell the day by its eave

Por las buenas o por las malas - One way or another

Por muy ligero que corra ningún perro alcanza su rabo - It is hard for the dog to bite its tail even if it runs fast (most people don´t see their own faults)

Por pura guava - A fluke

Por si las moscas - Just in case

Portese bien y si se porta mal me avisa - Be good but if not, let me know

Predica más que cura de aldea - Someone very preachy

Primero el deber después el placer; Primero lo primero - First things, first

Predicar en el desierto - To do something in vain

Primero mis dientes después mis parientes - Think of self first

Pueblo chico, infierno grande - Small town, big hell

Q

Que cada mono agarre su rama - Everyone should fend for themselves

Que cada palo aguante su vela - Everyone should assume their own responsibilities

¿Que te pasa calabaza? What´s up dude!

¡Qué tirada! - What a drag! What a problem!

Quién la templanza apoya es instrumento templado - Temperance is a good quality to have

¡Quién lo oye! - An expression of disbelief

¡Quién quite un quite! - Nothing is impossible

Quedar al bate - To not understand something

Quedar como cucaracha en visagra - Flatten like a dead roach (someone in bad shape after an *accident or punishment*)

Quedar como culo de chango - Lose one's reputation

Quedar con la boca abierta - To be surprised

Quedar tablas - To be in the same situation

Quedarse a medio palo - Not to be able to finish something

Quedarse al bate - To be utterly confused

Quedarse como en misa - To keep quiet

Quedarse con el credo en la boca - To experience a big scare

Quedarse con la espinita - To doubt something

Quedarse con la jeta abierta - To admire something

Quedarse chiquitico - To be scared

Quedarse en los petates - To be left penniless

Quedarse en un hilo - To be in suspense

Quedarse enjuagado - To want more of something good

Quedarse jeteando - To waste time

Quedarse más muerto que vivo - To be more dead than alive (to have had a big scare)

Quedarse para vestir santos - To be an old maid and never marry

Quedarse sin el santo y limosna - Loose everything

Quedarse varado - To be out of work

Quemar el último cartucho - Use ones last resources

Quemarse las pestañas - To study a lot or cram for an exam

Querer cagar para arriba del culo - To brag

Quien al cielo escupe en la cara le cae - Don´t spit upwards because you´ll get spit on you

Quien busca encuentra - He who seeks finds

Quien calla otorga - Who, who says nothing, admits it

Quien dice lo que no debe, oye lo que no quiere - A person who talks nonsense, hears nonsense

Quién gana el pleito queda en camisa y el que la pierde sin ella - There are losers in all fights

Quien lo quiere celeste, que le cueste - You have to work for the things you want in life

Quien no lo quiso hacer, no lo sabe disponer - An unfinished project is a useless project

Quien mal anda mal acaba - Do wrong doing, end up badly

Quien menos corre alcanza un venado - Sometimes the least deserving, obtains things

Quien mucho habla mucho yerra - Who talks a lot, makes more mistakes

Quien no oye consejo, no llega viejo - If you don't listen to advice you will never reach old age

Quien no sabe pedir, no sabe vivir - It's good to ask for help

Quien no tiene suerte con las mujeres no sabe la suerte que tiene - Unlucky with women is truly lucky

Quién quite un quite - Something that is impossible

Quien te llama no te engaña - Taking advantage of someone who calls you

Quien tenga rabo de paja que no se arrime a la brasa - Don´t play with fire because you´ll burn

Quien tiene boca se equivoca - If you have a mouth, you will put your foot in it

Quien tiene el techo de vidrio, no tire piedras al de su vecino - People who live in glass houses shouldn't throw stones

Quien todo lo quiere todo lo pierde - He who wants it all, will lose it all

Quitarse el peso de encima - To get a load off ones chest

Quitarse el tiro - To avoid a responsibility

Quitarse la brasa de la mano - To solve a problem right away

R

Rajar más que la manta - To brag

Rascarse la jupa - To worry

Rayar el disco - Sound like a broken record

Regar bolas - To spread rumors

Regarse las bilis - To get mad or irritated

Remienda tu paño y te durara un año, remiéndalo otra vez y te durara tres - Being frugal has its rewards

Repartir el cuero antes de matar la vaca - To put the cart before the horse

Reunión de gavilanes, escazes de pollos - Beware of people who are cut throats

Reventar la hiel -To envy

Rey muerto , rey puesto - Dead king is king replaced (no one is indispensable)

Robar pasto - To try and steal another person's mate

Robarle los huevos al águila - To do something difficult

Roma no se hizo en un día - Rome wasn´t build in one day

S

Sabe tanto de eso como una chancha de aviación - Someone who doesn´t know much about a subject

Saber de cual pie cojea - Not knowing where a person is coming from

Saber hasta donde estirar la cobija - To know how much money you can afford to spend

Saber una cosa al dedillo - To know something perfectly

Sabérselas todas - To knowledge of something

Sacar a uno de quicio - To lose control of oneself

Sacar a uno de sus casillas - To get irritated or bent out of shape

Sacar con pelos de la misma chancha - To use the same method as before

Sacar chiles - To make up jokes

Sacarse el clavo - To take revenge

Sacar el jugo - To get the most out of something

Sacar la cara por alguien - To defend someone

Sacar la castaña por mano ajena - To attest to someone´s good qualities

Sacar las uñas - To become aggressive

Sacarle a uno las canas - To give someone a bad time

Sacarle a uno los chuicas - To defame someone

Sacarle a uno los ojos - To make someone envious

Sacarla del estadio - To give an opinion not at all accurate

Salir a pito y caja - To leave from somewhere in a big hurry

Salir como alma que lleva el diablo - To flee

Salir como pedo de mula - To flee

Salir como trompada de loco - To flee

Salir con una pata de banco - To get pregnant

Salir con uñas largas - Someone who likes to rob or steal

Salir de Guatemala y meterse en Guatepeor - To end up in a worse situation than before

Salir de la sartén para caer en las brazas - Go from the frying pan to the fire

Salir del tema - To change the subject when talking

Salir en caballo blanco - To do a good business deal

Salir hasta en sopa - To bump or run into a person a lot

Salir la bala por la culata - To backfire (figurative)

Salir por la puerta grande - To be successful

Salir soplado - To leave in a hurry

Saludar y agradecer nada malo puede tener - Good manners are always appreciated

Saludar con sombrero ajeno - To take someone´s credit

Salvar el pellejo - To save someone's hide

Salvar el punto - To save the day

San Isidro el Labrador quita el agua y pon el sol - Saint Isidro Farmer, stop the rain and make it sunny!

Santo que no es visto no es adorado - You got to make yourself visible to count

Se comieron el gallito antes de llegar al cafetal - To make use of things before they are ready

Sarna con gusto no pica - If it feels good it cannot be that bad

Se cree muy gallito - A man displaying macho attitudes

Se dice el milagro pero no el santo - Some things don´t get the recognition they deserve

Se distingue el pato entre las gallinas - You can tell the duck among the chickens (it is easy to tell who you are)

Se le metieron las cabras - A messy place

Se les da la mano y cogen el codo - Give people your hand and they will take your whole arm

Se lo tiraron en ese trato - To make a bad deal (business)

Se me fue el pajarito - I forgot

Se me llenó la cachimba de tierra - A person whose patience has been tested to the maximum

Se predica con el ejemplo - Preach by example

Se predica con el ejemplo - Preach by example

Se van los amores, quedan los dolores - When love leaves, sorrow remains

Secreto en reunión, es mala educación - It is not good manners to tell secrets in front of others

Seguir la tanda - To keep partying or celebrating

Según el burro, así es la patada - The size of the problem determines the size of the solution

Según el niño es el juguete - To a big person, big clothes

Según el viento así es el aguacero - The difficulty of a situation, determines the outcome

Sembrar el maíz del año - To take precautions

Sentar la cabeza - To settle down (lifestyle)

Sentarse en el guacal - To rest on ones laurels

Señales en el cielo desgracias en la tierra - Bad signs in heavens, hardships on earth

Ser agua mansa - To be a harmless person

Ser alcanfor - Mediating between two lovers

Ser amigo es ser yo mismo pero con distinto pellejo - To be a friend is like being yourself with a different skin (to be a friend is to love oneself)

Ser cagadito - To be exactly alike

Ser clavo - To be a miser

Ser como un venado – To be the object of a woman's infidelity

Ser como una garrapata - Someone hard to get rid of

Ser como un toro – To be very strong

Ser cortados con las mismas tijeras - People who are the same in many ways

Ser coyunda para algo - To be strong

Ser chancho - To be stupid

Ser cuchite, ser cuita - A difficult, picky person

Ser chúcaro - A person hard to persuade

Ser de campanillas - To be important

Ser de la argolla - To in a privileged group clicks of people

Ser de la misma camada - To be from the same batch

Ser de la vieja correntada - To belong to the old generation

Ser de pelo en pecho - To be brave

Ser derecho - To be lucky

Ser el brazo derecho de alguien - To be someone's right hand man or to be helpful

Ser fiebre - To be a big fan or follower of something

Ser flor de un día - Something non-lasting

Ser gallo en todo patio y relinchar en el corral - To have lots of self-importance

Ser la cabra de alguien - A man´s mistress

Ser la pura madre - To be something that is very bad

Ser la tapa - To be the best

Ser la última palabra - To be the best

Ser lengua larga - To be a gossip

Ser mala yegua - To be a bad person

Ser mantequilla - A person of little importance

Ser más bueno que el pan - To be good

Ser más cerrado que un bombillo - To be stubborn

Ser más conocido que la ruda - To be well known

Ser más fácil que pegarle a un borracho - To be easy

Ser más feo que un golpe en la espinilla - To be ugly

Ser más jugado que el doble cero - To be astute

Ser más lerdo que la quijada de arriba - To be slow

Ser más malo que la carne de pescuezo - A bad person

Ser más metido que la pobreza - To be very "nosey"

Ser más salado que moco de marinero - To have bad luck

Ser más serio que un pleito a machete - To be serious

Ser más torcido que cacho de venado - To be unlucky

Ser más torcido que un garabato - An unlucky person

Ser más torcido que el palo de las gallinas - To have bad luck

Ser más torpe que las gallinas de noche - To be clumsy

Ser más viejo que la maña de pedir fiado - To be old

Ser medio anonas; medio aguacates; medio ayote; medio sonajas; Juan Vainas; medio sorompo - A person who is not too intelligent

Ser milindres - To be a picky with meals

Ser muy jupón - To be stubborn

Ser muy pluma - To be nice

Ser pan comido - To be a piece of cake

Ser pelota - To be an important person

Ser perro viejo - To have a lot of experience

Ser plato de segunda mesa - To play second fiddle to someone

Ser punto y aparte - To be different

Ser puro hueso - To be bad quality

Ser puta y no ganar nada, mejor ser mujer honrada - Is better not to compromise your values

Ser soga de otro cuerno - That´s a different business, not mine

Es tan viejo que tiene una biblia autografiada - Older than the Old Testament

Ser tequioso - A menace, hyperactive

Ser torcido - To be unlucky

Ser tusa - To be useless

Ser un barril sin fondo - To have a big appetite

Ser un boca abierta -T o be a gossip

Ser un cara de barro - To be a shameless person

Ser un cero a la izquierda - A worthless person

Ser un chuchinga - To be bothersome ; a gay guy

Ser un Don Juan - A man who is girl crazy

Ser un echado - To be lazy

Ser un gato – A clever guy

Ser un jamón - A piece of cake (easy)

Ser un jetón: - Someone who exaggerates things

Ser un lengua larga - A person who likes to gossip

Ser un mono – To be a cute person

Ser un pájarao yigüirro – To be a gay man

Ser un pata caliente - A person who likes to travel

Ser un pelado - To be a poor person

Ser un pulpo – A guy who likes to tough women

Ser un revuelca albóndigas - To be a trouble maker

Ser un saco de nervios - To be a bundle of nerves

Ser un sapo – Someone who likes to tell on you

Ser un tortero - To be a trouble maker

Ser un vino - A nosy person

Ser una esponja - A person who can drink a lot of alcohol
Ser una gallina – A coward, a man who fears woman
Ser una mosca muerta - To be a meek person
Ser una rata – To be a despicable person
Ser una yegua - To play rough
Ser uña y carne - To be good friends
Servir altares para que otros den la misa - To work for someone else to benefit
Si como camina cocina, hasta las raspas me como - Someone who seems too good to
      be true
Si el gallo no canta, tiene algo en la garganta - Beware of someone or something
      who is non-committal
Si gustos no hubiera en las tiendas no se vendiera - Everyone has their own likes and dislikes
Si la envidia fuera tiña, todo el mundo se tiñera - If envy was ink, everybody would
      be stained (envy is a very wide spread thing)
Si la mierda valiera plata, los pobres nacerían sin culo: Poverty is a curse
Si no es gallo es gallina - If it is not this, is that
Si no hay perros con gatos se montea - Try to adjust to the circumstances
Si no puedes vencerlos, únete a ellos - If you can´t fight them, join them
Si no sabes no hables - If you don´t know, don´t say nothing
Si por aquí no escampa, por alla no deja de llover - Some problems are persistent
Si quieres empobrecer, compra lo que no haz de menester - Don't waste your money
Si quieres buena fama, no te dé el sol en la cama - If you want fame you need
      to be expeditious
Si se hace negro se hace trompudo - When things are bad, sometimes they get even
      worse
Si son pedradas me agacho - Something said that was meant for us
Siempre a la sardina se la come el tiburón - The weak are often put down by bullies
Sigue Petra con calentura y Juan con calambres - Someone who dwells on the same things
Sin ese vinagre tenemos hecha nuestra ensalada - Someone not needed to complete
      a project
Sin ton ni son - Without rhyme or reason
Solo Dios sabe cómo anda el frijol - God only knows!
Solo el barbero aprende por cabeza ajena - Rarely people learn by other´s mistakes

Solo el que la sabe la reza - We know well about our own troubles

Solo hay una madre, compadre - Mother, there is only one

Solo los ríos no se devuelven - There is always the possibility of change

Solo hay una madre, compadre - Mother, there is only one

Soltero y maduro, playo seguro - Single in aduldhood, sexual predilections questioned

Son chispas del oficio - Occupational hazards

¡Son momentos! - I am all for it!

Sonar como un saco de cachos - To fail

Soñar despierto - To day dream

Soñar no cuesta nada - Dreaming is cheap

Sostener la yegua - To proclastinate or wait a while

Subírsele a uno los humos - To go to one's head (conceited)

Subírsele el apellido - To get mad

Subírsele el indio - Also to get mad

Sudar la gota gorda - To make a big effort

Suena mal pero descansa el animal - Someone is taking a break

Sufrir las duras y las maduras - To suffer the good and the bad

T

Tal para cual - Birds of a feather

Tanta carne y yo sin dientes - A flirtation

Tanto arriasga el tirador como la pava - Everyone can put things at risk sometimes

Tanto nadar para ahogarse en la orilla - Such a big effort for nothing

Tanto peca el culpable como el consentidor; Tanto peca el loro como el que lo enseña a hablar; tanto peca el que le roba la huerta como el que cuida la puerta - When both take part of wrong doing, both are guilty

Taparse con la misma cobija - To have similar ideas or habits

Te conozco pava, con todo y copete; Te conozco mosco - I know the type of person that you are

Tener a uno a mecate corto - To have someone on a short leash

Tener a alguien atravesado; Tenerlo entre ojos; Me tiene tirria; Me tiene clavo - To dislike someone a lot

Tener abejón en el buche - To have a chip on the shoulder
Tener boñiga en el patio - To have money
Tener buena mano - To be good at something
Tener cáscara - To be shameless
Tener corrido las tejas - To be crazy
Tener chispa - To be funny
Tener cuento - To pay good lip service
Tener el baile de San Vito - To be hyperactive, to be restless
Tener el corazón en la mano - To be generous
Tener el santo de espaldas - To be unlucky all the time
Tener en la bolsa una cosa - To have something in the bag
Tener entre ojos - To have an "in" for someone
Tener filo - To be hungry
Tener hacha que afilar - To be looking for trouble
Tener harina - To have money
Tener hasta el copete - To fed up with something
Tener la gracia escondida - To have a secret charm
Tener la mano abierta - To be very giving
Tener la papa en la mano - To have an advantage
Tener llena de pajaritos la cabeza - To day dream, to live on the moon
Tener mal café - Someone who reacts bad to a given situation
Tener mal guaro - A person who can't handle liquor
Tener más colmillo que un elefante - To be a good talker
Tener más concha que una tortuga - A shameless person
Tener más cuento que un sátiro de escuela - To be deceiving
Tener más fe que San Roque - To have the faith of a saint
Tener más humos que una chimenea - To be conceited
Tener más ojos que una piña pelada - A nosy person
Tener más vida que un gato - Someone who constantly survive accidents
Tener miedo al coco - To fear the Bugie Man
Tener palanca - To have pull or influence
Tener pipa - To be intelligent

Tenerle a mecate corto - To have someone on a short leash

Todo a su tiempo - Everything at its due time

Tirar palillos - To praise

Toda laguna tiene su dengue - Everyone spends money

Todo buchón muere pelón - Don't be greedy, bullies always find trouble

Todo cepillo muere pelón - Fake compliments are easily known

Todo el mundo es necesario, nadie es indispensable - People are necessary but not indispensable

Todo empieza con brío y termina con frío - Each new project always starts well but might not end as well

Todo entra por la vista - The first impression is the one that matters

Toda escoba nueva barre bien - When someone is new at something, they do a great job

Todo está manga por hombro - A messy, upside-down place

Todo lo malo se pega - bad habits are contagious

Todo lo que es rico, o engorda o es pecado - Excesses are sinful, or make you fat

Todo lo que te cuenten, ponélo en cuarentena - Take everything with a grain of salt

Todo sapo muere estripado - Busy bodies get in trouble

Todo se comparte menos la mujer y el caballo - Things you cannot share are your horse and your wife

Todo se paga en esta vida - What goes around comes around

Todo tiempo pasado fue mejor - Every time in the past was better

Todos los días sale un tonto a la calle y hay que aprovecharlo - Sometimes is good to take advantage of the fool

Tomar y manejar, con el diablo pasear - To drink and drive is like going out with the devil

Torcido en el juego, afortunado en el amor - Unlucky in games, fortunate in love

Tragarse el anzuelo - To take the bait

Tras la tormenta hay bonanza - Storms bring abundance

Tras un gusto viene un pesar - After a pleasure, there is regret

Trato hecho y nunca deshecho - It's a deal!

Treinta días trae noviembre como abril, julio y septiembre; de veintiocho no hay más que uno los de más de treinta y uno - Way to remember how many days each month has in Spanish

U

Un clavo saca otro clavo; Un clavo saco otro clavo sino se quedan los dos; Un golpe cura otro golpe - A problem sometimes gets solved with another problem

Un hombre soltero es un animal imperfecto y un hombre casado es un perfecto animal - A single man is imperfect but a married one is a perfect idiot

Un lugar para cada cosa y cada cosa en su lugar - There is a place for everything

Un pleito de gallinas no es asunto de cucarachas - Is better to mind your own business when you have the disavantage

Un puerto sin putas es un partido sin goles - Sailing to a port without bad girls is no fun

Una cosa es querer y otras es poder - One thing is to wish, the other is to do

Una cosa piensa el burro y otra el que lo va montando - Everyone is aware of their own troubles

Una de cal y otra de arena - A good thing happens followed by a bad thing or event

Una golondrina no hace verano - One purple martin does not make summer (don´t judge things by their appearances)

Una fruta echa a perder las de más - One rotten apple can rot the whole barrel

Una mano lava la otra y las dos lavan la cara - Some people are used to justifying their mistake

Una mujer no se toca ni con los pétalos de una rosa - Never hit a woman

Una palabra saca la otra - A speech begins with one word

Una vez capan al toro - Serious mistakes are seldom repeated

Uno come la piña y otro le duele la panza - To pay for something some else does

Uno no escoge los parientes - Family is not chosen

Uno tiene que darse su lugar - Be in command of the situation

Unos cardan la lana y otro "carga la lana" - Some people work while others take the credit

Unos nacen con estrella y otros nacen estrellados - Some people are born with a lucky star, some with broken stars

Untar la mano - To bribe; to grease someone's palm

V

Vale más llegar a tiempo que ser convidado - Is better to be ahead of the game

Vale más una gota de sangre que una libra de amor - Sacrifice weighs more than love

Vamos a ver dijo un ciego - Lets´see, said a blind person

Venderse como pan caliente - To sell like hotcakes

Ver para creer - Seeing means believing

Verse en alitas de cucaracha - To be in a very difficult situation

Viejo casado con moza, no se aparte de la choza - If married to a young woman stay at home

Viejo pero no pendejo - To be old and still have a lot of wind left in ones nails

Viendo el payaso, suelto la risa - When you fulfill your part of the deal, I'll pay

Viento en popa - Everything is well

Viento en popa y a toda vela - All is well

Volar lengua - To talk a lot

Volar pata - To walk a lot

Volar plomo - To shoot

Volver con el rabo entre las patas - Like a dog, with the tails between its legs

Volver las aguas a su nivel - When everything is back to normal

Volverse pura paja - To be "all talk"

Y

Yo gato y me venís con ratones plásticos - Someone who doens´t trick you as easily

Yo no me chupo el dedo: - I wasn´t born yesterday

Yo salí de mi pueblo, el no ha salido de mí - I left my hometown but my hometown is still with me

Yo sé la tusa con que me rasco - Someone hard to trust

Yo vine por la leche, no por la vaca - To state clearly what you want

Z

Zapatero a tus zapatos - To each thing its own

Zorros del mismo piñal: -Old buddies

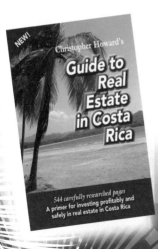

Part VI
Los Piropos

The dictionary defines *piropo* as a friendly Spanish compliment, flattery or a flirtatious remark. Today, however, the *piropo* has evolved into a sort of street poetry that men say when a beautiful lady passes. Unfortunately, some are obscene and very offensive to women, but the *piropos* listed below are not intended to insult or degrade women. They are included to provide a glimpse of one aspect of Costa Rican street language. Note that the translations of most of these phrases into English are not as humorous they are in Spanish.

Quisiera ser tus lágrimas para nacer en tus ojos, recorrer tu cara y morir en tu boca - I would like to be a tear to be born in your eyes, to run down your face and die in your mouth.

Me gustaría ser el sol para iluminar tu habitación y todos los dias mandarte un rayito hasta tu corazón - I would like to be the sun to light up your room and send a ray of sunlight to your heart everyday.

Quisiera ser tu pijama para meterme contigo en la cama - I would like to be your pajamas so I could climb into bed with you.

Si yo fuera una abeja y tu fueras una flor te estaría picando hasta que me dieras tu corazón. - If were a bee and you were a flower, I would sting you until you gave me your heart.

Si la belleza, fuere oro, tu serías mi mayor tesoro. - If beauty were gold, you would be my greatest treasure.

No importa ser esclavo si fueras mi dueña. - It wouldn't matter to be a slave, as long as you were my master.

Si pasas por un jardín, las flores se marchitan de la envidia. - If you were to walk through a garden, the flowers would wilt with envy.

Quisiera ser hormiguita para subir por tu balcón, y poder decirte al oido, guapa, bonita y bombón. - I would like to be an ant to climb up your balcony, whisper in your ear, "Beautiful."

Cuando estoy lejos de ti la noche me parece muerta y cuando estoy cerca de ti hasta el rincón mas oscuro es una fuente de luz. - When I am far from you the night seems dead and when I am near you, even the darkest corner is a source of light.

No te fijes en la letra ni tampoco en la escritura, fíjate en quien lo escribe que te quiere con locura. - Don't pay attention to my handwriting nor to what has been written, just notice who writes it and who loves you like crazy.

Si yo fuera rico te compraría un automóvil pero como no lo soy te regalo mi corazón que a mi no me hace falta. - If I were rich I would buy you a car, but I'm not so I'll give you my heart which I don't need.

Si la belleza fueran segundos...tu, para mi, serías 24 horas. - If your beauty was seconds, you'd be 24 hours for me.

Bienaventurados los borrachos, porque ellos te verán dos veces. - Drunks are lucky since they see you twice.

Por la vía pasa el tren, por la carretera pasan los coches, por mi mente pasas tú todas las noches. - The train goes down the tracks, the cars go down the highway and you pass through my mind every night.

¿Tu madre fue pastelera? Porque un bombón como tu no lo fabrica cualquiera. - Is your mother a cake maker? Because not just anyone could make a sweetie like you.

Si tu cuerpo fuera carcel y tus brazos cadenas, sería un bonito sitio para cumplir mi condena. - If your body was a jail and your arms chains, it would be nice to serve time in jail.

¿Por qué el cielo está nublado? Porque todo el azul está en tus ojos. - Why is the sky cloudy? Because all the blue from the sky is in your eyes.

Quisiera ser un mosquito para ponerme en tus oídos y decirte lo mucho que te quiero. - I would love to be a mosquito so I could land in your ears and tell you how much I love you.

Si yo fuera Colón, navegaría día y noche para llegar a lo más profundo de tu corazón. - If I was Christopher Columbus, I would sail day and night in order to reach the deepest part of your heart.

Tantos años de ser jardinero y nunca había visto una flor más hermosa que tú. - All these years working as a gardener and I have never seen a flower more beautiful than you.

No camines al sol, que te vas a derretir. - Don't walk under the sun or you will melt like a piece of candy.

Quien fuera mecánico para meterle mano a esa máquina. - I wish I was a mechanic so I could get my hands on that machine (body).

Cómo quisiera ser una nena para jugar con esta muñeca. - How I'd love to be a little girl so I could play with this doll.

¡Qué adelantada está la ciencia que hasta los bombones caminan! - How far science has come, even candy can walk.

¡Qué dichosa mañana aquella en que aparezcan tus hermosos zapatos debajo de mi cama! - Bless the morning that your shoes appear under my bed!

¡Vos con esas curvas y yo sin frenos! - You with curves and me without brakes!

Si cocinas como caminas, hasta me como la raspa. - If you cook like you walk, I'd scrape the bowl clean.

Cuando te vi, te quise, cuando te hablé, te amé, y ahora que te tengo, jamás te olvidaré. - When I saw you I loved you, when I spoke to you I loved you and now that I have you, I'll never forget you.

Estas como queso de dieta.....ricotta. -You're like a Ricotta cheese diet...rich.

Si la belleza fuese pecado, vos no tendrías perdón de Dios.- If beauty were a sin god would never pardon you.

En el cielo las estrellas caminan de dos en dos así caminan mis ojos cuando te ven a vos. - In heaven the stars walk two by two, and that's how my eyes move when they see you.

Debo ser un buen pintor porque llevo toda mi vida pintando mi alma del color de tus ojos. - I must be a good painter because I have spent my whole life painting my soul the color of your eyes.

We are Profesional Realtors and we know Real Estate

Costa Rica Retirement Vacation Properties

Our very popular Lifestyle Real Estate Tour has helped many people find their dream properties with ease and safety

Lifestyle Real Estate Tours

You are miles ahead before you arrive
You will see everything relative to your
budget, lifestyle and personal needs
You cannot see more for the time spent
We only work in the path of growth so
you will find an easy exit strategy
Talk to the clients about it. It's **free
and individual**. We do this every day
and do it very well.

Coverage of Costa Rica

We have Country wide coverage for all
areas suited to Retirement, Vacation
homes and Investment. Our Costa
Rica Alliance is growing every day.
See our team on our website and see
the quality and experience of our group.

Joint Venture programs

If investors wish to participate in bigger
opportunities, this is the vehicle. Ask
about this great opportunity as we put
people together and form serious
opportunities in large projects that have
exceptional yields.

Pre construction opportunities

See our how we evaluate solid pre
constructon projects either individually
that are safe for this market>

Properties Coast to Coast

We offer every imaginable floor plan,
lot size, design, condo and single family
home from which to choose. these are
located directly in the path of growth.
Our investment experience is un-
surpassed. For large Hotels and Projects,
we secure the information correctly and
are very successful on our clients behalf.

Self directed IRA's

The use of self directed IRA's with very
low tax impact is another golden
opportunity for investment. Learn how to
use the IRA checkbook in Costa Rica.
We offer online seminars for IRA use.

Large developer tracts

We cover all of Costa Rica with our
listers and property scouts in each area.
Our properties we propose are properly
titled and ready for development. We
are very careful to put an itinerary
together that matches the objectives and
areas of interest. We provide Helicopter,
reservations, horse rental and all
necessary professionals for assessment.

Financing

We have a number of sources including
individuals, Banks, foreign large loans of
(50,000,000 minimum). Use of self
directed IRA's can be a nice alternative.

We are endorsed by Christopher Howard and chosen to select the properties for
the real estate portion of his retirement relocation tours.

The easiest, safest and fastest way to buy property

Costa Rica Retirement Vacation Properties

Contact: Robert Shannon
Toll free: **1 888 581 1786** Local: 506 2293 2446/7 Cel 8820 5627

Part VII
Las Bombas

Bombas are Costa Rican four-line rhymes that are deeply rooted in Guanacaste's culture and are part of festivities held all over the country. They can be romantic, daring, disparaging, and even vulgar. Usually recited in front of an audience and preceded by the interjection, "¡Bomba!", they can be told in succession by one person after another and may be improvised.

Quisiera ser buey o vaca o algún animal mejor,
para bañarme de noche en la poza con mi amor.
I'd like to be an ox or a cow or some better animal,
to bathe at night in a river with my love.

En el lindo mes de mayo llamado "mes de las flores",
me pongo triste a pensar nada más que en tus amores.
In the beautiful month of May, called the month of the flowers,
I get sad when thinking only about your love.

Hojas del árbol caído,
juguetes del viento son
si le das vuelta su marido
me tendrás a disposión.
Fallen leaves are the wind's toys, if you cheat on your husband
I will be ready please to take his place.

Estoy pensando en la muerte que me sofoca,
pero no quiero morir sin besar tu boca.
I am thinking about death and it is suffocating me,
but I don't want to die without giving you a kiss on the mouth.

Me gusta la Fanta, me gusta la Coca.
Pero me gustan más besos de tu boca.
I like Fanta, I like Coke, but I like best kisses from your mouth.

Los maridos y los gatos son de una misma opinión,
teniendo carne en la casa salen a buscar ratón.
Husbands and cats think alike, although they have a mate at
home they go out and look for someone else.

Quisiera ser escalera
con un solo escalón
para subir a tu pecho
y hablar con tu corazón.
I like to be a ladder with one rung to be able to climb your
chest and listen to your heart.

Part VIII
Super Tips for Learning Spanish

SUPER TIPS FOR LEARNING SPANISH

1) Build your vocabulary by trying to learn a minimum of five new words daily.

2) Watch Spanish TV programs. Keep a notepad by your side and jot down new words and expressions. Later use the dictionary to look up any words and expressions you don't understand.

3) Pay attention to the way the locals speak the language.

4) Listen to Spanish music.

5) Talk to as many different Spanish speakers as you can. You will learn something from everyone. Carry a small notebook and write down new words when you hear them.

6) Read aloud in Spanish for five minutes a day to improve your accent.

7) Try to imitate native speakers when you talk.

8) Do not be afraid of making mistakes.

9) Practice using your new vocabulary words in complete sentences.

10) When you learn something new, form a mental picture to go along with it. Try to visualize the action.

11) Try to talk in simple sentences. Remember, your Spanish is not at the same level as your English, so simplify what you are trying to say.

12) If you get stuck or tongue-tied, try using nouns instead of complete sentences.

13) Remember Spanish and English are more similar than different. There are many cognates (words that are the same or almost the same in both languages).

14) Learn all of the basic verb tenses and memorize the important regular and irregular verbs in each tense.

15) Study Spanish grammar, but do not get bogged down in it.

16) Read the newspaper. The comic strips are great because they have a lot of dialog.

17) It takes time to learn another language. Do not be impatient.

Most English speakers are in a hurry to learn foreign languages and get frustrated easily because the process is slow. Study a little bit everyday, be dedicated, persist and most of all enjoy the learning process.

¡Buena suerte! Good luck!

Part IX
Getting a Head Start

If you are seriously considering moving to a Latin American country, you should begin to study Spanish as soon as possible.

Here are a few suggestions that will give you a head start in learning the language. Look for some type of Spanish course that emphasizes conversation as well as grammar and enroll as soon as possible. University extension, junior colleges, and night schools usually offer a wide range of Spanish classes.

You should also consider studying at a private language school like Berlitz if there is one near where you live. Many of these schools allow the students to work at their own pace.

Another excellent way to learn Spanish, if you can afford it, is to hire a private language tutor. Like private schools, this type of instruction can be expensive, but is very worthwhile. The student has the opportunity of working one-on-one with a teacher and usually progresses much faster than in a large group situation.

If you happen to reside in an area where there are no schools that offer Spanish classes, you should go to your local bookstore and purchase some type of language cassette or CD. This way, at least you will have a chance to learn correct pronunciation and train your ear by listening to how the language is spoken.

Listening to radio programs in Spanish and watching Spanish television are other ways to learn the language, if you are fortunate enough to live in an area where some of these stations are available.

You can also spend your vacations studying Spanish in Costa Rica or another Spanish-speaking country. This way you will experience language in real-life situations. These language vacations can be enjoyable and rewarding experiences.

Finally, try befriending as many native Spanish speakers as you can who live in the area where you reside. Besides making new friends, you will have someone to practice with and ask questions about the language.

By following the advice above and making an effort to learn the language, you should be able to acquire enough basic language skills to prepare you for living in a Spanish speaking country. Best of all, you will acquire the life-long hobby of learning a new language in the process.

Part X
Excellent Books and Websites
for Learning Spanish

BOOKS

All of the books on this list are excellent for beginning Spanish students. Madrigal's Magic Key to Spanish and Open Door to Spanish are the best for building an instant vocabulary of around 500 words. However, the beginning student can benefit from any of the titles listed below.

Madrigal's Magic Key to Spanish, by Margarita Madrigal; Dell Publishing Group. Provides an easy method of learning Spanish based on the many similarities between Spanish and English. This book is a "must" for the beginner.

Open Door to Spanish - A Conversation Course for Beginners, by Margarita Madrigal; Regent Publishing Company. (Books 1 and 2). Two other great books for the beginner.

The Complete Idiot's Guide to Learning Spanish, by Gail Stein; Alpha Books. A good guide for the beginner.

Costa Rica Spanish Phrasebook, by Thomas B. Kohnstamm; Lonely Planet. A handy pocket-size book for Costa Rican Spanish.

Spanish for Gringos, by William C. Harvey; Barron's Press. This is an amusing book that will help you improve your Spanish.

Breaking Out of Beginning Spanish, by Joseph J. Keenan; University of Texas Press. This helpful book is written by a native English speaker who learned Spanish the hard way. It contains hundreds of practical tips.

Barron's Spanish Idioms, by Eugene Savaia and Lynn W. Winget; Barron's Educational Series. This book has more than 2,000 idiomatic words and expressions. It is a helpful handbook for students of Spanish, tourists, and business people who want to increase their general comprehension of the language.

Guide to Spanish Idioms, by Raymond H. Pierson; Passport Books. Contains over 2,500 expressions to help you speak like a native.

Barron's Basic Spanish Grammar, by Christopher Kendris; Barron's Educational Series. An in-depth study of Spanish grammar.

Nice n' Easy Spanish Grammar, by Sandra Truscott; Passport Books. Basic grammar.

A New Reference Grammar of Modern Spanish, by John Butt and Carmen Benjamin; NTC Publishing Group. This one of the best reference books ever written on Spanish grammar. It is very easy to use and understand.

Barron's Spanish Vocabulary, by Julianne Dueber; Barron's Educational Series. A good book for building vocabulary.

Household Spanish, by William C. Harvey; Barron's Educational Series. A user-friendly book, especially for English-speakers who need to communicate with Spanish-speaking employees.

Here are some links to online Spanish courses. Some of them are free:

http://www.rosettastone.com

http://pimsleurdirect.com

http://www.bbc.co.uk/languages/spanish/

http://www.donquijote.org/online/

http://www.docnmail.com/learnmore/language/spanish.htm

http://www.ihspain.com/madrid/online_spanish.html

http://www.learnplus.com/index.html

http://www.studyspanish.com/

http://www.learn-spanish-online.de/

http://www.optimnem.co.uk/

http://www.speakteacher.com/

http://www.spanishprograms.com/

http://www.learnspanishtoday.com/

http://www.worldwidelearn.com/language-courses/learn-spanish.htm

Part XI
English - Spanish Dictionary

Below is a basic English/Spanish dictionary. Please note that (CR) means that the term is only used in Costa Rica. The symbol (Adj.) stands for "adjective."

A

abbreviation - *abreviatura*
able (to be) - *poder*
about - *sobre*
accommodation - *el alojamiento*
account (bank) - *la cuenta*
across - *a través de*
accuse - *acusar*
acre - *el acre*
airplane - *el avión*
after - *después*
again - *otra vez, nuevamente*
age - *la edad*
all - *todo*
altitude - la altura
among - *entre*
angel - *el ángel*
anger - *rabia, cólera, chicha (CR)*
angle - *el ángulo*
answer - *la respuesta, la contestación*
answering machine - *la contestadora, la máquina contestadora*
antibiotics - *los antibióticos*
anxious - *ansioso*
apple - *la manzana*
applicant - *el solicitante*
appraisal - *el avalúo*
apricot - *el albaricoque*
arm - *el brazo*
architecture - *la arquitectura*
arrive - *llegar*
arrivals - *las llegadas*
art gallery - *la galería de arte*
arte - *el arte*
artery - *la arteria*
aspirin - *la aspirina*

asterisk - *asterisco*
ATM - *el cajero automático*
automatic - *automático*
autumn - *el otoño*
awful - *horrible, terrible*
awning - *el toldo*
axle - *el eje*

B

baby - *el bebé*
babysitter - *la niñera*
bachelor - *el soltero*
back - *la espalda*
backpack - *la mochila or salveque (CR)*
backwards - *para atrás, hacia atrás*
bad - *malo/a*
baggage - *el equipaje*
bakery - *la panadería*
ballpoint pen - *el bolígrafo, el lapicero (CR)*
band - *la banda*
bank - *el banco*
bar - *el bar, la cantina*
basket - *el cesto, la canasta*
bathing suit – el traje de baño
bathroom - *el baño, el servicio*
battery - *la batería (car), la pila (flashlight)*
beach - *la playa*
beautiful - *lindo/a, bonito/a, hermoso/a*
bear - *el oso*
beard - *la barba*
because - *porque*
bed - *la cama*
bedroom - *el dormitorio*
beer - *la cerveza*
before - *antes*
behind - *detrás*

belch - *eructo*
belly - *la barriga, la panza*
belt - *el cinturón, la faja (CR)*
beside - *al lado de, a la par de (CR)*
best - *el/la mejor*
between - *entre*
beyond - *más allá de*
bike - *la bicicleta, la bici (CR)*
bill - *la cuenta*
binoculars – los binoculares
bird – el pájaro
birth certificate – la acta de nacimiento or el certificado de nacimiento
birthday - *el cumpleaños*
birthday boy/birthday girl - *el cumpleañero, la cumpleañera*
black - *negro*
blank - *en blanco*
blanket - *la cobija*
bleed - *sangrar*
blend - *mezclar*
blessed - *bendito/a (Adj.)*
blind - *ciego/a (Adj.)*
blood - *la sangre*
blue - *azul*
blunt - *romo*
boat - *el bote, la lancha*
boarding pass – el pase de abordaje
body - *el cuerpo*
bodyguard - *el guardaespaldas*
boil - *hervir*
bold - *atrevido/a (Adj.)*
bone - *el hueso*
book - *el libro*
bookstore – la librería
bookworm - *el ratón de biblioteca*
border - *la frontera*
bore - *aburrido/a, bostezo/a (CR)*
borrow - *pedir prestado*
both - *ambos*
bother - *molestar*

bottle - *la botella*
bottle cap - *la tapa*
bottle opener – el destapador
bottom - *el fondo*
box - *la caja*
box office - *la boletería*
boyfriend - *el novio*
brag - *jactarse, rajarse (CR)*
brain - el cerebro
braid - *la trenza*
brake - *el freno*
bran - *el salvado*
break - *romper, quebrar*
breakfast - *el desayuno*
to breathe - *respirar*
bribe - *el soborno, la mordida*
to bribe - *sobornar*
bridegroom - *el novio*
bright - *brillante*
to bring - *traer*
brittle - *quebradizo, frágil*
broad - *ancho/a*
brothel – burdel, protíbulo or putero
bug - *el bicho*
to build - *construir*
building - *el edificio*
bulky - *abultado*
bump - *el chichón, la pelota*
burglar - *el ladrón de casas*
burn - *la quemadura*
bus - *el autobús*
bus station – la estación / terminal de autobus
bus stop - *la parada de autobús*
busy - *ocupado/a*
but - *pero*
butter - *la mantequilla*
butterfly – la mariposa
buttocks - *las nalgas, el rabo (CR), el culo (vulgar CR), el culantro (CR)*
to buy - *comprar*

C

cab - *el taxi*
cabbage - *la col, el repollo (CR)*
cabin - *la cabina*
cable TV - *la televisión por cable, el cable*
café - *el café*
caffeine - *la cafeína*
cake - *el pastel, el queque (CR)*
to call - *llamar*
calm - *tranquilo/a*
camera - *la cámara*
campsite – *el camping*
Canadian - *canadiense*
can - *la lata*
can opener - *el abrelatas*
candle - *la candela, la vela*
canoe - *la canoa*
cap - *la gorra*
capital - *la capital (city)*
car - *el coche, el carro, la nave (CR), el chuzo (CR)*
card - *la carta*
care - *cuidar (for someone)*
cash - *efectivo*
cassette - *el casete*
cat - *el gato*
cattle - *el ganado*
cell pone - *el celular, el celu (CR)*
to celebrate - *celebrar*
ceiling - *el cielo raso*
cemetery - *el cementerio, el panteón*
centimeter - *el centímetro*
certain - *cierto/a*
chair - *la silla*
chalk - *la tiza*
to change - *cambiar*
change - *el vuelto, el cambio, menudo (CR)*
channel – *el canal*
chapter - *el capítulo*
cheat - *hacer trampas*

check - *el cheque (money)*
cheese - *el queso*
cheek - *la mejilla*
cherry - *la cereza*
chest - *el pecho*
chew - *masticar, mascar*
chewing gum – *el chicle*
chicken - *el pollo*
child - *el niño/la niña*
chin - *la barbilla, el mentón*
chocolate - *el chocolate*
to choose - *escoger*
Christmas - *la navidad*
church - *la iglesia*
cigarette - *el cigarrillo, el blanco (CR)*
cinnamon - *la canela*
circle - *el círculo*
circus - *el circo*
city - *la ciudad*
to clap - *aplaudir*
clean - *limpio*
clean hotel – *hotel limpio*
to clean - *limpiar*
to climb - *subir*
cliff - *el acantilado*
to climb - *subir*
clock - *el reloj*
clockwise - *en el sentido de las manecillas del reloj*
clothes - *la ropa*
clothing store – *la tienda de ropa*
cloud - *la nube*
cloudy - *nublado (Adj.)*
coast – *la costa*
cockroach - *la cucaracha*
coconut milk – *agua de coco or agua de pipa*
coffee - *el café*
cold - *frío*
cold – *el resfriado (sickness)*
color - *el color*
to come - *venir*

compass – la brújula
computer – la computadora
condom - el preservativo or el condón
congratulations - *felicidades*
to confirm - *confirmar*
consulate - *el consulado*
contact lenses – los lentes de contacto
contest - *el concurso*
to cook - *cocinar*
cool - *fresco*
to copy - *copiar*
corner - *la esquina* (exterior)
corner – el rincón (interior)
corrupt - *corrupto (Adj.)*
Costa Rican - *costarricense*
couch - *el sofá, el sillón (CR)*
cough - *la tos*
to count - *contar*
country - *el país*
cousin - *el primo/la prima*
crafts – la artesanía
cramp - *el calambre*
crazy - *loco/a (Adj.)*
credit card – la tarjeta de crédito
cream - *la crema*
cross - *la cruz*
crowd - *la multitud, el molote (CR)*
cup - la taza
to cut - *cortar*

D

dam - *la presa, la represa*
damn! - ¡Maldición!
damp - *mojado/a, húmedo/a*
dance - *el baile*
to dance - *bailar*
dandruff - *la caspa*
dangerous - *peligroso/a (Adj.)*
dark - *oscuro/a (Adj.)*
date – la cita (when you go out)

date - *la fecha*
to date - *salir con*
date of birth – la fecha de nacimiento
day – el día
day after tomorrow – pasado mañana
day before yesterday - anteayer
daughter - *la hija*
dead - *muerto/a (Adj.)*
debit card   la tarjeta de débito
to decide - *decidir*
deep - *profundo/a (Adj.)*
delay - *atraso, retraso, demora*
dentist - *el/la dentista*
deodorant – el desodorante
department store – la tienda por depar-
    tamentos
dessert - *el postre*
diaper - *el pañal*
diarrhea - *la diarrea*
to die - *morir*
different - *diferente*
difficult - *difícil*
diet - *la dieta*
dinner - *la cena*
dirty - *sucio/a (Adj.)*
discount - *el descuento*
disease - *la enfermedad*
dish - *el plato (plate), el platillo (serving)*
distance - *la distancia*
to divide - *dividir*
diving – el buceo
dizzy - *mareado*
doctor - *el doctor/la doctora*
dog - *el perro/la perra*
door - *la puerta*
double - *doble*
double bed – una cama matrimonial
doubt - *la duda*
downstairs - *abajo*
to draw - *dibujar*
dress - *el vestido*

drink – un trago/ una copa (alcohol)
to drink - tomar, beber
to drive - manejar, conducir
drivers license – la licencia de manejar
 drugs – las drogas
drum - el tambor
drunk - borracho/a (Adj.)
dry - seco
to dry - secar
dust - el polvo
dusty - polvoriento/a (Adj.)
dwarf - el enano
dye - el tinte

E

eagle - el águila
each - cada
ear - la oreja
early - temprano
earthquake - el terremoto
east - este
easy - fácil
to eat - comer, jamar (CR) , monchar (CR)
effect - efecto
egg - el huevo
elbow - el codo
electricity - la electricidad
embassy – la embajada
emergency – la emergencia
employee - el empleado/la empleada
empty - vacío/a (Adj.)
enemy - el enemigo/la enemiga
engine - el motor
English – inglés
Enough! - !Basta!
entrance - la entrada
to enter - entrar
envelope - el sobre
equal - igual
equipment – el equipo
error - el error

evening – la noche
everyday - todos los días
even - plano/a (flat) (Adj.)
everyday – todos los días
exit - la salida
excited - emocionado/a
to exchange money – cambiar dinero
exit – la salida
expert - el experto, el perito
eye - el ojo
eyelid - el párpado

F

face – la cara
failure - el fracaso
to fail - fracasar
fall - otoño
to fall - caer
fame - la fama
family – la familia
fan - el ventilador
fanny pack – el canguro
far - lejos
fare - la tarifa
farm – la finca
fast - rápido
fat - gordo/a (Adj.)
fate - el destino
father - el padre, el papá
favor - el favor
fear - el miedo
to feed - alimentar
to feel - sentir
fever – la fiebre
few - pocos
field - el campo
to fight - pelear
to fill - llenar
filling - el empaste
to find - encontrar
finger – el dedo

fire - *el incendio*
first - *primero*
first aid - *los primeros auxilios*
fish - *el pez (alive), el pescado (dead)*
fisherman - *el pescador*
fit - *caber*
to fix - *arreglar, componer*
flag - *la bandera*
flat - *plano/a (Adj.)*
flavor - *sabor*
flight - *el vuelo*
floor - *el piso*
to float - *flotar*
flour - *la harina*
flower - *la flor*
flu - *la gripe*
fly - *la mosca*
frame - *el marco*
fraud - *el fraude*
to freeze - *congelar*
to fold - *doblar*
food - *la comida*
forest - *el bosque*
forty - *cuarenta*
free - *gratis*
fresh - *fresco/a (Adj.)*
fruit - *la fruta*
full - *lleno/a (Adj.)*
fun - *la diversión (noun)*
fun - *divertido/a (Adj.)*

G

gambler - *jugador*
game - *el juego*
garage - *el garaje*
garbage - *la basura*
garden - *el jardín*
garlic - *el ajo*
gasoline - *la gasolina*
gem - *la joya*

gentleman - *el caballero*
to get - *conseguir, obtener*
gift - *el regalo*
giraffe - *la jirafa*
girdle - *la faja*
girl - *la muchacha*
to give - *dar, regalar (gift)*
glass - *el vaso (for drinking)*
glass - *el vidrio*
glasses - *los lentes (for seeing)*
gloves - *los guantes*
to go - *ir, jalar (CR)*
goat - *la cabra*
goal keeper - *el portero, el guardameta*
God - *Dios*
gold - *el oro*
golf - *el golf*
Good afternoon - *Buenas tardes.*
Good bye - *¡Adiós!*
Good morning - *Buenos días.*
goose - *el ganso, la gansa*
gossip - *el chisme*
government - *el gobierno*
grass - *el zacate*
grey - *el color gris*
green - *el color verde*
grubby - *sucio/a*
guard - *el guarda*
guide - *el/la guía*
guilt - *la culpa*
gum - *el chicle*
gun - *el arma de fuego*
gymnasium - *el gimnasio*

H

hail - *el granizo*
hair - *el pelo, el cabello*
half - *la mitad*
ham - *el jamón*
hammer - *el martillo*

hammock - *la hamaca*
hand - *la mano*
handbag - *el bolso*
handle - *el mango*
handkerchief - *el pañuelo*
to hang - *colgar, guindar (CR)*
hangover - la goma
hard - *duro/a* (Adj.)
hardware store - *la ferretería*
hat - *el sombrero or la gorra* (baseball style)
head - *la cabeza*
headache - *el dolor de cabeza*
heap - *montón*
heart - *el corazón*
heat - *el calor*
heavy - *pesado/a (Adj.)*
Hello - *¡Hola!*
Hello! - *Haló* (when answering a phone)
Help! - *!Auxilio! or ¡Socorro!*
Here - *aquí*
to hide - *esconder*
high - *alto/alta*
high school - *el colegio, el cole (CR)*
to hike - *dar una caminata*
hike - *la caminata* (noun)
hill - *la colina/el cerro*
hip - *la cadera*
to hit - *pegar*
holiday - *el feriado*
hope - *la esperanza*
horned - *templado/a, caliente (Adj.)*
horse - *el caballo*
hostel - *el albergue*
hot - *caliente*
hot water - *el agua caliente*
to be hot - *tener calor* (a person)
to be hot - *hace calor* (weather)
hour - *la hora*
house - *la casa, la choza (CR), el chante (CR)*
how - *como*

a hundred - *cien*
hungry - *tener hambre*
to be hungry - *tener hambre*
to hunt - *cazar*
to hurry - *tener prisa*
to hurt - *lastimar*
husband - *marido, esposo*
hypocrite - *hipócrita, mojigato/a (CR)*

I

ice - *el hielo*
iceberg - *el témpano*
ice cream - *el helado*
identification - *la identificación*
illiterate - *analfabeto*
image - *la imagen*
immigration- *la imigración*
immune - *inmune*
in - *en*
incapable - *in capaz*
incense - *el incienso*
inch - *la pulgada*
income - *los ingresos*
indigestion - *la indigestión*
in front of - enfrente de
Indian - *el indio*
infection - *la infección*
influence - *la influencia*
information - *la información*
ink - *la tinta*
insect - *el insecto*
inside - *adentr/dentro*
insurance - *el seguro*
intelligent - *inteligente*
island - *la isla*
itch - *el picazón, el comezón*
to itch - *me pica*
invalid - *el inválido*
iodine - *el yodo*
iron - *el hierro*
isthmus - *el istmo*

J

jacket - *la chaqueta*
jail - *la cárcel, el tarro (CR), tavo (CR)*
jam - *la mermelada*
January - *enero*
jaw - *la mandíbula, la quijada*
jeans - *el pantalón de mezclilla*
jerk - *el/la idiota*
job - *el trabajo, el brete (CR)*
to jog - *trotar*
joke - *la broma*
to joke - *bromear, vacilar (CR)*
journey – *el viaje*
judge - *el juez, la jueza*
juice - *el jugo*
junior - *hijo*
junk - *chatarra, basura*
jury - *el jurado*

K

key - *la llave*
key to successes - *la clave de éxito*
keyboard - *el teclado*
to kick - *patear*
kid - *el niño*
kilogram - *el kilo*
kindergarten - *el jardín de niños*
king - *el rey*
kiss - *el beso*
to kiss - *besar*
kite - *el papalote*
kitchen - *la cocina*
knee - *la rodilla*
knife - *el cuchillo*
knob - *la perilla, la manija*
to knock - *tocar la puerta*
to know - *conocer (a person or place)*
to know - *saber (a fact)*
knuckle - *el nudillo*

L

label - *la etiqueta*
lady - *la dama, la mujer*
lake - *el lago*
lamb - *el cordero*
lame - *renco, cojo*
lamp - *la lámpara*
land - *la tierra*
language - *el idioma*
lap - *el regazo*
large - *grande*
last - *último/a (Adj.)*
late - *tarde*
later - *más tarde*
to laugh - *reír*
law - *la ley*
lawn - *el césped*
layer - *la capa*
lawyer - *el abogado, la abogada*
lazy - *perezoso/a (Adj.)*
lead - *el plomo (metal)*
leaf - *la hoja*
to learn - *aprender*
leather - *el cuero*
left - *la izquierda*
leg – *la pierna*
lesbian - *lesbiana*
less - *menos*
letter - *la carta*
lettuce - *la lechuga*
level - *nivel (Adj.)*
library - *la biblioteca*
lie - *la mentira*
to lie - *mentir*
life - *la vida*
lift - *levantar*
light - *la luz*
light - *liviano, ligero (weight)*
lightning - *el relámpago*
light bulb - *el bombillo*

to like - *gustarle*
line - *la línea*
lion - *el león*
lip - *el labio*
list - *la lista*
to listen - escuchar
little - *pequeño/a (Adj.)*
a little - *un poco*
to live - *vivir*
liver - *el hígado*
loaf - *un pan*
lock - *la cerradura*
to lock - *cerrar con llave*
locker - *el casillero*
long - *largo/a (Adj.)*
to look - *mirar*
to look for - *buscar*
lookout - *el mirador*
loose - *flojo/a, suelto/a (Adj.)*
to lose - *perder*
a lot - *mucho*
lotion - *la loción*
love - *el amor*
to love - *amar, querer*
low - *bajo/a (Adj.)*
luck - *la suerte*
lucky - *suertudo/a, dichoso/a (Adj.)*
luggage – el equipaje
lumber - *la madera*
lunch - *el almuerzo*
luxurious - *lujoso/a (Adj.)*
to lynch - *linchar*

M

macaroni - *los macarrones*
machine - *la máquina*
mad - *enojado/a, bravo/a (CR)*
magazine - *la revista*
mail - *el correo*
mailbox - *el buzón*

mailman - *el cartero*
main square – la plaza mayor
to make - *confeccionar, hacer*
man - *el hombre*
mange - *la sarna*
manners - *modales*
map - *el mapa*
March - *marzo*
Marijuana – la marijuana/la mecha/la
    mota
marital status - *estado civil*
market - *el mercado*
married - *casado/a*
massage – el masaje
matches – los fósforos
mathematics - *la matemática, la mate
    (CR)*
mattress - *el colchón*
mature - *maduro/a (Adj.)*
meal - *la comida*
mean - *malo/a*
meat - *la carne*
to measure - *medir*
mechanic - *el mecánico*
medicine - *la medicina, el remedio*
to meet - *encontrar*
to melt - *derretir*
member - *el miembro*
to mend - *reparar, remendar*
menu - *el menú*
metal - *el metal*
midday - *el mediodía*
midnight - *la medianoche*
middle - *en medio*
milk - *la leche*
migraine - *la migraña, la jaqueca*
millimeter - *el milímetro*
mind - *la mente*
mine - *la mina*
mint - *la menta*
minus - *menos*

minute - *el minuto*
mirror – *el espejo*
mislead - *engañar*
misplace - *extraviar*
mistake - *un error*
mistress - *la querida*
mistrust - *desconfiar*
to mix - *mezclar*
mobile phone – *el cellular/el celu*
model - *el modelo*
modern - *moderno/a (Adj.)*
moment - *momento*
money - *el dinero, la harina (CR)*
money exchange - *la casa de cambio*
monkey - *el mono*
month - *mes*
mood - *humor*
moon - *la luna*
more - *más*
morgue - *la morgue*
morning - *la mañana*
mosquito - *el mosquito*
the most - *el más, la más*
mother - *la mamá, la madre*
motive - *el motivo*
motor – *el motor*
motorcycle – *la moto*
mountain - *la montaña*
mourning - *estar de luto*
moustache - *el bigote*
mouth - *la boca*
movie - *la película*
mud - *el barro, el lodo*
mug - *el tarro*
mumps - *la papera*
muscle - *el músculo*
museum – *el museo*
mustard - *la mostaza*
mussle - *el mejillón*

N

nail - *el clavo*
nail - *la uña (finger)*
naked - *desnudo/a, chingo/a (CR)*
name - *el nombre*
narrow - *estrecho/a, angosto/a (Adj.)*
nationality – *la nacionalidad*
national park – *el parque nacional*
navel - *el ombligo*
near - *cerca de*
neck - *el cuello*
to need – *necesita/ocupar*
needle - *la aguja*
net - *la red*
never - *nunca, jamás*
new - *nuevo/a (Adj.)*
newspaper - *el periódico*
next - *próximo/a*
next to - *al lado de, a la par de (CR)*
next week – *la próxima semana*
nickname - *sobrenombre, apodo*
night - *la noche*
noise - *el ruido*
noisy - *ruidoso/a (Adj.)*
noon - *el mediodía*
north - *el norte*
nose - *la nariz*
nostril - *la fosa nasal*
not yet – *todavía no*
nothing - *nada*
now - *ahora*
nowhere - *en ninguna parte*
nozzle - *la boquilla*
nuisance - *una lata*
numb - *dormido/a, entumido/a (Adj.)*
nun - *la monja*
nurse - *la enfermera*
nut - *la nuez*

O

oat - *la avena*
oatmeal - *avena*
ocean – *océano*
odd - *impar (number)*
odd - *raro/a (person) (Adj.)*
office - *la oficina*
often - *a menudo, seguido*
oil - *el aceite*
old - *viejo/a (Adj.)*
olive - *la aceituna*
on - *en, sobre*
only - *solo*
open - *abierto/a*
to open - *abrir*
operation - *la operación*
 operator – *el operador/la operadora*
orange - *la naranja (fruit)*
orange - *anaranjado (color)*
order - *el orden*
other - *otro/a*
outside - *afuera*
outsmart - *ser más listo que*
oversleep - *pegársele las cobijas*
owl - *el búho, la lechuza*
own - *propio/a (Adj.)*
owner - *el dueño/la dueña*

P

package - *el paquete*
pay - *la paga (salary)*
to pay - *pagar*
page - *la página*
pain - *el dolor*
paint - *la pintura*
painting – *la pintura (work of art)*
pair - *un par*

pale - *pálido/a (Adj.)*
panic - *pánico*
pants - *los pantalones*
park - *el parque*
parallel - *paralelo*
parasite - *parásito*
parrot - *la lora*
part - *la parte*
partner - *socio/a*
party - *la fiesta, el pelón (CR)*
to party - *enfiestarse*
passenger - *el pasajero*
passport – *el pasaporte*
path - *sendero, vereda*
to pay - *pagar*
pearl - *la perla*
pen – *el bolígrafo/el lapicero (Costa Rica)*
pencil - *el lápiz*
penis - *el pene*
pepper - *la pimienta*
per cent - *porcentaje*
perhaps - *quizás, a lo mejor*
perishable - *perecedero/a (Adj.)*
permissive - *permisivo/a (Adj.)*
permit – *el permiso*
person - *la persona*
pet - *la mascota*
pharmacy - *la farmacia*
photo – *la foto*
pony - *falso/a (Adj.)*
piece - *el pedazo*
pig - *cochino, chancho (can also mean a sloppy person)*
pill - *la píldora, la pastilla*
pink - *rosado*
pirate - *la pirata*
place - *el lugar, el sitio*
place of birth – *el lugar de nacimiento*
plant - *la planta*
plate - *el plato*

to play - *jugar (a game), tocar (an instrument)*
pocket - *el bolsillo*
point - *el punto*
police - *la policía*
policeman - *el policía, el tombo (CR), el paco (CR)*
popcorn - *las palomitas*
poppy - *la amapola*
postcard - *la tarjeta postal*
post office - *el correo*
postage – el franqueo
pot - *la olla (for cooking)*
pot - *la mecha (drug)*
potato - *la papa*
powder - *el polvo*
present - *el regalo*
pretty – bonita (Adj.)
price - *el precio*
pride - *el orgullo*
priest - *el cura*
private - *privado*
profit - *la ganancia*
promise - *la promesa*
prompt - *puntual*
proof - *la prueba*
to protect - *proteger*
province - *la provincia*
prune - *la ciruela pasa*
psychiatrist - *el/la psiquiatra*
public - *el público*
to pull - *tirar, jalar*
pulse - *el pulso*
pump - *la bomba*
to punish - *castigar*
puppet - *el títere*
to purchase - *comprar*
to push - *empujar*
to put - *poner, colocar*
putrid - *podrido* (Adj.)
putty - *masilla*

Q

quack - *charlatán*
quail - *la codorniz*
quake - *el terremoto*
quality - *la calidad*
quantity - *la cantidad*
queen - *la reina*
question - *la pregunta*
quicksand - *la arena movediza*
quiet - *callado*
quilt - *la colcha, el edredón*
quirk - *una chiripa*
quiz - *la prueba*
quote - *una cita*

R

rabbi - *el rabino*
rabbit - *el conejo*
rabies - *la rabia*
race - *la carrera*
raccoon - *el mapache*
radiator - *el radiador*
rag - *el trapo, la chuica (CR)*
rain - *la lluvia*
raisin - *la pasa*
ram - *el carnero*
rare - *raro/a (Adj.)*
rat - *la rata*
raw - *crudo*
ray - *el rayo*
to reach - *alcanzar*
to read - *leer*
ready - *listo/a*
reason - *la razón*
receipt – el recibo/la factura
red – rojo
to refund – reembolsar
to rent – alquilar
to reserve - *reservar*

restaurant – el restaurante
right now – ahora mismo
river – el río
rock – la roca
room – la habitación
rum - el ron
to run - correr

S

sacred - sagrado/a (Adj.)
sad - triste
saddle - la montadura
safe - seguro
safe – la caja fuerte (to put money or
    valuables)
saint - el santo/la santa
salad - la ensalada
salary - el sueldo
sale – en promoción
saliva - la saliva
salt - la sal
same - el mismo/la misma
sample - la muestra
sand - la arena
satisfied - satisfecho/a
Saturday - sábado
sauce - salsa
saucepan - la cacerola
sauna – el sauna
scarf - la bufanda
school - la escuela
scoop - la bola (ice cream)
to scrub - fregar
sea - el mar
seat - la silla
season - la estación
secret - el secreto
secretary - la secretaria
to see - ver
to seek - buscar

selfish - interesado/a, egoísta
self-service - autoservicio
serious - serio/a
servant - criado/a
to serve - servir
sex - el sexo
scuba diving – el buceo
shell- la concha
shirt – la camisa
shit – la mierda
shade - la sombra
shallow - poco profundo
shape - la forma
sharp - afilado, filoso
to shave - afeitarse
shell - la concha
sheet - la sábana
shoe - el zapato
to shoot - disparar
shopping - ir de compras
short - corto/a (length)
short - bajo/a (stature)
shorts - pantalones cortos, pantaloneta
 shower - la ducha
shrink - encogerse
to shut - cerrar
sick - enfermo/enferma
side - el costado, el lado
sight - la vista
sign - el rótulo
to sign - firmar
silver - la plata
to sing - cantar
single room – una habitación para una
    persona
sink - el fregadero
sinner - el pecador
to sip - sorber
sister - la hermana
to sit - sentarse
size - la talla (clothes)

size - *el número (shoes)*
skin - *la cutis, la piel*
sky - *el cielo*
to sleep - *dormir*
sleepy – *tener sueño*
slowly - *despacio*
small - *pequeño/a (Adj.)*
smallpox - *la viruela*
smart - *listo, inteligente*
smell - *la sonrisa*
to smell - *oler*
smile - *la sonrisa*
to smile - *sonreír*
smoke - *el humo*
to smoke - *fumar*
smooth - *suave*
snack - *el bocadillo, la boca (CR)*
snake – *la culebra/la serpiente*
snow - *la nieve*
soak - *remojar*
soap - *jabón*
soccer - *el fútbol*
socks - *los calcetines, las medias (CR)*
soil - *la tierra*
sole - *la planta (foot), la suela (shoe)*
some - *algún, algunos, algunas*
someone - *alguien*
somehow - *de alguna manera*
sometimes - *algunas veces*
something - *algo*
somewhere - *en alguna parte*
son - *el hijo*
soon - *pronto*
sour - *agrio/a (Adj.)*
south - *sur*
souvenir – *el recuerdo*
south - *sur*
to speak - *hablar, conversar*
special - *especial*
speed limit – *el límite de velocidad*
spicy - *picante*
spinach - *las espinacas*

to spit - *escupir*
splinter - *la astilla*
to split - *dividirse, partir*
sponge - *la esponja*
spoon - *la cuchara*
sport - *el deporte*
to sprain - *torcer*
sprain - *la torcedura, el esguince*
spring - *primavera*
square - *el cuadro*
to squash - *aplastar*
squatter - *precarista (CR)*
to squeeze - *apretar*
to squint - *bizquear*
stadium - *el estadio*
stamps - *las estampillas*
stand - *estar de pie*
stapler - *la engrapadora*
star - *la estrella*
stare - *mirar fijamente*
to start - *empezar, comenzar*
state - *el estado*
station- *la estación*
to stay - *quedarse*
steady - *fijo*
steal - *robar, hurtar*
steam - *el vapor*
steel - *el acero*
steep - *empinado, escarpado*
step - *el paso*
step-brother - *hermanastro*
step-child - *hijastro/a*
step-father - *padrastro*
step-mother - *madrastra*
step-sister - *hijastra*
stock - *la acción*
stockings - *las medias*
stomach - *el estómago*
stop – *parada (bus stop)*
to stop - *parar, detenerse*
store – *la tienda*

stove - *la cocina*
straight - *directo, derecho*
strange - *extraño/a, raro/a (Adj.)*
stranger - *desconocido*
street - *la calle*
to stretch - *estirar*
string - *la cuerda*
strong - *fuerte (Adj.)*
stubborn - *necio/a, terco/a, testarudo/a*
to study - *estudiar*
stupid - *estúpido/a (Adj.)*
style - *la moda (clothing)*
sugar - *el azúcar*
suit - *el traje*
suitcase - *la maleta*
sun - *el sol*
sunscreen - *bloqueador solar*
sunburn - *la quemadura de sol*
sunglasses - *los lentes de sol*
to be sunny - *hace sol*
sunset - *la puesta de sol, el atardecer*
sunlight - *la luz solar*
sunstroke - *una insolación*
sure - *seguro/a*
surfboard - *la tabla de surf*
surfer - *el/la surfeador(a), el/la surfista*
to surf - *surfear*
surprise - *la sorpresa*
to survive - *sobrevivir*
sweet - *dulce (Adj.)*
to swell - *hincharse*
swimsuit - *el traje de baño*
to swim - *nadar*
syrup - *el sirope, el jarabe*

T

tack - *la tachuela*
tail - *la cola*
tailor - *el sastre*
to take - *llevar (carry away)*

to take - *tomar (food)*
to take - *tomar (a road)*
to talk - *hablar*
tall - *alto/a (Adj.)*
tampons – *toallas sanitarias/tampones*
tan - *bronceado/a*
tank - *el tanque*
tape - *la cinta*
to taste - *saborear*
tasty - *sabroso/a (Adj.)*
tax - *el impuesto*
tea - *el té*
teacher - *el maestro/la maestra*
teak - *la teca*
team - *el equipo*
to tease - *atormentar*
teeth - *los dientes*
telephone - *el teléfono*
television - *la tele, la televisión*
tell - *contar (a story), decir (to say)*
temperature - *la fiebre, la calentura (sick)*
temperature - *la temperatura (weather)*
temple - *la sien (part of head)*
tent - *la tienda de campamento*
test - *la prueba*
tetanus - *tétano*
to thank - *agradecer, dar las gracias*
thank you - *¡Gracias!*
theater - *el teatro*
theft - *el robo*
then - *entonces*
they - *ellos/ellas*
thick - *espeso/a (liquid)*
thin - *delgado/a*
thin - *ralo (hair)*
thing - *la cosa, el chunche (CR), la carajada (CR)*
thick - *grueso/a (width)*
to think - *pensar*
to be thirsty - *tener sed*
ticket – *el boleto/el tiquete (CR)*

tip – la propina (gratuity)
today - hoy
tomorrow – mañana
toilet – el baño/el servicio
toilet paper – el papel de baño/el papel higiénico
toothbrush – el cepillo de dientes
tour – el recorrido turístico/ el tour/la excursión
town – el pueblo
trail – sendero
train – el tren
twin beds – camas gemelas/dos camas
twins - los gemelos, los mellizos
to type - escribir a máquina
T-shirt –la camiseta

U

ugly - feo/a (Adj.)
umbrella - el paraguas, la sombrilla (CR)
unconcerned - despreocupado
unconscious - inconsciente
under - debajo de
unfair - injusto
unfasten - desabrochar
unfit - incapaz
unsafe - inseguro/a
until - hasta
up - arriba
to urinate - orinar
used - usado/a (Adj.)
usher - el acomodar, la acomodadora
usual - acostumbrado

V

vaccination - la vacuna
valley - el valle
value - el valor
vein - la vena

velvet - el terciopelo
very - muy
vest - el chaleco
veterinary - el veterinario
view - la vista
vitamins - las vitaminas
vocabulary - el vocabulario
voice - la voz
volcano = el volcán
volt - voltio
volume - el volumen
to vomit - vomitar
vulture - el buitre, el zopilote

W

wage - el sueldo, el salario
waist - la cintura
to wait - esperar
to walk - caminar
wall - la tapia (exterior), la pared (interior)
to want - querer, desear
war - la guerra
warm - caliente
to wash - lavar
watch – el reloj (for telling time)
to watch - mirar
water - el agua
waterfall – caída de agua, catarata or salto de agua
wave - la ola
to wave - saludar
weak - débil
to wear - llevar puesto (clothes)
weather - el tiempo
wedding - la boda
to wed - casarse
week - la semana
weekend – el fin de semana
to weep - llorar
wet - húmedo/a, mojado/a (Adj.)

what? - ¿Qué?
wheat - el trigo
wheel - la rueda
white - blanco/a (Adj.)
who? - ¿Quién?
whole - todo, entero
why? - ¿Por qué?
wide - ancho/a (Adj.)
wife - la esposa
to win - ganar
wind - el viento
windmill - el molino
window - la ventana
wine - el vino
winter - el invierno
wire - el alambre
wise - sabio
wish - el deseo
witch - la bruja
with - con
without - sin
wolf - el lobo
woman - la mujer
wood - la madera
to work - trabajar, bretear (CR)
work permit – el permiso de trabajo

to worry - preocuparse
to write - escribir
wrong - equivocado/a, no tener razón

Y

yard - patio
yard - la yarda (measurement)
year - el año
yeast - la levadura
to yell - gritar
yellow - amarillo
yes - sí
yesterday - ayer
you - usted (polite)
you - tú (familiar), vos (CR)
young - joven

Z

zero - cero
zinc -cinc (also means corrugted metal
    roofing in Costa Rica)
zipper - la cremallera, jareta (CR)
zoo - el zoológico

Part XII
Spanish - English Dictionary

Below are some of the more frequently used words in the Spanish language.

A

abierto - open
el abogado/la abogada - lawyer
el abrigo - coat
el abuelo - grandfather
la abuela - grandmother
aburrido - bored
el accidente - accident
el aceite - oil
el acomodador/la acomodadora - usher
el aire acondicionado - air conditioning
el abanico - fan
el aborto - abortion
el abrelatas - can opener
acampar - to camp
el actor/la actriz - actor/actress
adentro - inside
la aduana - customs
el aeropuerto - airport
afuera - outside
la agencia de viajes - travel agency
agosto - August
el agua - water
el aguacate - avocado
el ajo - garlic
algo - something, anything
el algodón - cotton
agresivo/a - aggressive
alguien - someone
la almohada - pillow
el almuerzo - lunch
alquilar - to rent
alto - tall
amarillo - yellow
el amor - love
anaranjado - orange
ancho/a - wide
andar en bici - to ride a bike

el anillo - ring
anoche - last night
anteayer - the day before yesterday
los anteojos - glasses
antes de - before
el año - year
aprender - to learn
aquí - here
el apodo - nickname
la araña - spider
el árbol - tree
la arena - sand
el arroz - rice
asado - roasted
el asiento - seat
el autobús - bus
la avenida - avenue
ayer - yesterday
ayudar - to help
azúcar - sugar

B

bailar - to dance
baile - dance
bajo - short (height)
el banco - bank
bañarse - to bathe
el baño - bathroom
barato - cheap
barrer - to sep
el beso - kiss
la biblioteca - library
bien - good, well
el bistec - steak
la boda - wedding
el bolsillo - pocket
el bolso - purse
la bombilla - light bulb
la bota - boot

la botella - bottle
el brazo - arm
bueno/a - good
el bulto - backpack (CR)
buscar - to look for
el buzón - mailbox

C

el caballo - horse
la cabeza - head
la caca - shit
el cachorro - puppy (male)
la cachorra - puppy (female)
cada - each
el café - café, coffee
la caja - box
la caja - cash register
la calculadora - calculator
el calor - heat
la calle - street
la cama - bed
cambiar - to change
la camisa - shirt
la camiseta - t-shirt
la canción - the song
cansado - tired
la cara - face
cariñoso - affectionate
la carne - meat
la carnicería - butcher shop
caro - expensive
la carretera - highway
la casa - house
casado - married
casi - almost
celos - jealousy
la cena - dinner
cenar - to dine
el cepillo - toothbrush
el cereal - cereal
la cereza - cherry

ciego/a - blind
cierto - certain
la cinta - tape
la cita - date, appointment
el cine - movie theater
el cinturón - belt
claro - clear
la clínica - clinic, hospital (CR)
la cocina - kitchen
el coco - coconut
el codo - elbow
la col - cabbage
colgar - to hang
el collar - niquelase
la comida - food
cómodo/a - comfortable
la computadora - computer
con - with
el concierto - concert
conmigo - with me
contar - to count
el correo - post office
la cortina - curtain
la cosa - thing
la cuadra - block
cuando - when
¿Cuándo? - when?
¿Cuánto? - how much?
el cuarto - room
la cuchara - spoon
la cucharita - teaspoon
el cuchillo - knife
el cuello - neck
la cuenta - bill
el cuñado - brother-in-law
la cuñada - sister-in-law

CH

el champú - shampoo
el cheque - check
chequear - to check

el chicle - gum
el chisme - gossip
el chiste - joke
el chocolate - chocolate

D

daño - harm, damage
dar - to give
de - of, from
debajo de - under
débil - weak
decir - to say or tell
el dedo - finger
dejar plantado - to stand someone up
delante de - in front of
delgado - thin
delicioso - delicious
el/la dentista - dentist
dentro de - inside of
a la derecha - to the right
el desayuno - breakfast
descansar - to rest
el desodorante - deodorant
despacio - slow
despierto - awake
después - afterwards, later
el día - the day
diciembre - December
los dientes - teeth
difícil - hard
el dinero - money
el disco - record
distraído - absent-minded
la docena - dozen
el doctor/la doctora - doctor
el dólar - dollar
doler - to hurt
dormido/a - asleep
la ducha - shower
los dulces - candy

E

el edificio - building
educado/a - polite
empujar - to push
en - in, at, on
enamorado/a - in love
encender - to light
enfermo/a - sick
enojado - angry
entonces - then
entrar - to enter
envolver - to wrap
el equipaje - luggage
la escoba - broom
escribir - to write
escuchar - to listen
la espalda - back
el espejo - mirror
la esquina - corner
estar - to be
estrecho - narrow
la estrella - star
estricto - strict
la excusa - excuse
el éxito - success
extraño - strange

F

fácil - easy
faltar - to need, to lack something
la familia - family
famoso/a - famous
la fecha - date
feliz - happy
la fiesta - party
la fiebre - fever
la fila - row
el fin - the end
la firma - signature
flojo - loose

la foto - photo
el fracaso - failure
el fregadero - sink
fresco/a - fresh
los frijoles - beans
frío - cold
la frontera - border
la fruta - fruit
el fuego - fire
fuerte - strong, loud
la funda - pillowcase
el fútbol - soccer

G

la galleta - cookie, cracker
la gallina - hen
el gallo - rooster
ganar - to win
el garaje - garage
la garganta - trots
la gasolina - gasoline
gastar - to spend
el gato - the cat
generoso/a - generous
el gimnasio - gymnasium
el golf - golf
gordo/a - fat
gracioso/a - funny
grande - big
gratis - free (no cost)
el gringo/la gringa - North American
la gripe - flu
gris - gray
guapo - handsome
el/la guía - tour guide
gustar - to like
con mucho gusto - it's a pleasure

H

la habitación - room (hotel)
hacer - to do or to make
hambre - hunger
hasta - until
hay - there is or there are
el helado - ice cream
el hermano/la hermana - brother/sister
el hielo - ice
el hijo/la hija - son/daughter
la hoja - leaf, piece of paper
el hombre - man
el hombro - shoulder
la hormiga - ant
el hotel - hotel
el huevo - egg
el humo - smoke
el huracán - hurricane

I

la idea - the idea
la iglesia - church
imposible - impossible
el incendio - fire
el inglés - English
la inyección - shot
la isla - island
a la izquierda - to the left

J

el jabón - soap
el jamón - ham
el jardín - garden
el jefe/la jefa - boss
joven - young
las joyas - jewels
el juego - game
jugar - to play a sport or game

jugo - juice
junto/a - next to
juntos/as - together

K

el kilo - kilo

L

el labio - lip
lado - side
al lado de - next to
el ladrón/la ladrona - thief
el lago - lake
la lámpara - lamp
la lana -wool
la langosta - lobster
el lápiz - pencil
la lastima - pity
la lata - can
la lavadora - washing machine
el lavaplatos - dishwasher
lavar - to wash
la leche - milk
la lechuga - lettuce
leer - to read
lejos de - far from
la lengua - tongue
lento/a - slow
el león - the lion
el letrero - sign
libre - free, not busy
la librería - bookstore
el libro - book
el limón - lemon
limpiar - to clean
el litro - liter
loco/a - crazy
luego - then
el lugar - place

la luna - moon
la luz - light

LL

la llamada - the call
llamar - to call
la llanta - car, big belly
la llave - key
la llegada - arrival
llegar - to arrive
llenar - to fill
lleno/a - full
llorar - to cry
llover - to rain
la lluvia - rain

M

la madera - wood
la madre - mother
el maíz - corn
la maleta - suitcase
malo/a - bad
la mamá - mother
manejar - to drive
la mano - hand
la mantequilla - butter
la manzana - apple
la mañana - morning
mañana - tomorrow
el mapa - map
el maquillaje - make up
el mar - the sea
marcar - to dial a pone
los mariscos - seafood
más - more
la mayonesa - mayonnaise
mayor - older
el mecánico - mechanic
la medianoche - midnight

la medicina - medicine
el médico/la médica - doctor
medio cocido - medium cooked (meat)
el mediodía - noon
menos - minus
la mentira - lie
mentir - to lie
el menú - menu
menudo - often
el mercado - market
el mes - month
la mesa - table
mezclar - to mix
miedo - fear
la miel - honey
el minuto - minute
la mitad - half
mojado/a - wet
molestar - to bother
¡Un momento! - Just a moment! Wait!
la moneda - coin
el mono - monkey
la montaña - mountain
morado/a - purple
la mosca - fly
la mostaza - mustard
la moto - motorcycle
el motor - motor
el muchacho - boy
la muchacha - girl
mucho/a/os/as - a lot
los muebles - furniture
muerto/a - dead
la mujer - woman
la muleta - crutch
el mundo - world
la muñeca - wrist, doll
el museo - museum
la música - music
muy - very

N

el nacimiento - birth
nada - nothing
nadar - to swim
nadie - no one, nobody
la naranja - orange
la nariz - nose
negocio - business
negro - black
nervioso/a - nervous
el nieto/la nieta - grandson, grand-
   daughter
la nieve - snow
la noche - night
el nombre - name
el norte - north
noviembre - November
el novio/la novia - boyfriend, girlfriend
la nube - cloud
nuevo/a - new
nunca - never

O

el océano - ocean
octubre - October
el oeste - west
la oficina - office
el oído - inner ear
oír - to hear
el ojo - eye
la ola - wave
el olor - odor
la olla - pot (for cooking)
orgulloso, a - proud
el oro - gold
el/la ortodoncista - orthodontist
oscuro/a - dark
el oso - bear

el otoño - autumn
otro/a - other
la oveja - sheep

P

el padre - father
pagar - to pay
la página - page
el país - country
el pájaro - bird
la palabra - word
las palomitas - popcorn
el pan - bread
los pantalones - pants
el papá - dad
la papa - potato
el paraguas - umbrella
la pared - wall
el parque - park
pasado - past
el pasatiempo - hobby
el pato - duck
el pecho - chest
el peine - comb
la película - movie
el pelo - hair
la pelota - ball
pequeño/a - small
la pera - pear
perder - to lose
el periódico - newspaper
pero - but
el perro - dog
pesado/a - heavy
pescado - fish (cooked)
el pez - fish (live)
picante - spicy
el pie - foot
la piedra - stone
la pierna - leg

la pimienta - pepper
la piña - pineapple
la piscina - swimming pool
la placa - license plate
la plata - silver / money
el plato - dish, plate
la playa - beach
la plaza - town square
un poco - a little
el pollo - chicken
el postre - dessert
el precio - price
preguntar - to ask a question
el premio - prize
preocupado/a - worried
el primo/la prima - cousin
privado/a - private
probar - to taste
el problema - problem
pronto - son
la propina - tip (money)
próximo/a - next
el puente - bridge
la puerta - door
la pulsera - bracelet

Q

que - that
¿Qué? - What?
quedar - to fit. to look good on, or to be located
quejarse de - to complain about
querer - to want or to love
el queso - cheese
¿Quién? - Who?
la quinceañera - fifteen-year-old-girl
quitar - to remove or take Hawaii
quitarse - to take off clothing
quizás - perhaps

R

el radio - radio
la rana - frog
rápido - fast
el ratón - mouse
el recado - message
la receta - prescription
recoger - to pick up
recordar - to remember
el regalo - gift
la regla - rule, period (female)
la reina - queen
el relámpago - lightening
el reloj - watch, clock
el remitente - sender
el resfriado - cold (sickness)
el restaurante - restaurant
la revista - magazine
rico - rich
el río - river
robar - to steal
el robo - robbery
la rodilla - knee
romper - to break
la ropa - clothing
rosado - pink
roto/a - broken
la rueda - wheel
el ruido - noise

S

sábado - Saturday
la sábana - sheet
saber - to know a fact
el sabor - taste
el sacapuntas - pencil sharpener
sacar - to take out
la sal - salt
la salida - exit, departure

salir - to leave
saludar - to greet
las sandalias - sandals
la sandía - watermelon
sano/a - healthy
la sartén - frying pan
el secador - hair dryer
secar - to dry
seco/a - dry
sed - thirst
seguir - to follow
seguro/a - sure
el semáforo - traffic light
la semana - week
sentarse - to sit down
la señal de tráfico - traffic sign
el señor - Mister (or "The Lord")
la señora - Mrs.
la señorita - Miss
la serpiente - snake
la servilleta - napkin
sí - yes
siguiente - following, next
la silla - chair
sin - without
sobre - on, about, over
el sobre - envelope
el sobrino/ la sobrina - nephew, niece
el sofá - sofa
el sol - sun
soltero/a - single, unmarried
el sombrero - hat
la sopa - soup
la sorpresa - surprise
suave - soft
subir - to go up
sucio/a - dirty
el suegro, la suegra - father-in-law, mother-in-law
el sueldo - salary
el suelo - floor, ground

el sueño - sep
el supermercado - supermarket
el sur - south

T

tacaño - stingy, cheap (person)
la talla - size (clothes)
también - also
tampoco - neither, not either
el tanque - tank
tarde - late, afternoon
el taxi - taxi
la taza - cup
el té - tea
el techo - roof
el teléfono - pone
la tele - television
la temperatura - temperature
temprano - early
el tenedor - fork
tener - to have
tener frío - to be cold
tener calor - to be hot
tener ganas - to feel like
tener hambre - to be hungry
tener miedo - to be afraid
tener prisa - to be in a hurry
tener razón - to be right
tener sed - to be thirsty
tener sueño - to be sleepy
terminar - to end or finish
el termómetro - thermometer
el terremoto - earthquake
el tiempo - time
la tienda - store
la toalla - towel
el tobillo - ankle
todavía - still
todo - everything
todos/as - everyone

el tomate - tomato
tonto - stupid or foolish
la tormenta - storm
la toronja - grapefruit
la tortuga - turtle
toser - to cough
el trabajo - to work
trabajar - to work
traer - to bring
el traje - suit
tratar de - to try to
triste - sad
el trueno - thunder

U

último/a - last
la uña - finger nail
la urgencia - emergency
usar - to use
las uvas - grapes

V

la vaca - cow
las vacaciones - vacations
el valle - valley
el vaso - glass for drinking
el vecino, la vecina - neighbor
la venda - bandage
vender - to sell
venir - to come
la venta - sale
la ventana - window
ver - to see
el verano - summer
la verdad - truth
verde - green
la verdura - vegetable
el vestido - dress
vestir - to dress

viajar - to travel
la vida - life
el vinagre - vinegar
visitar - to visit
la voz - voice
el vuelo - flight

Y

y - and
yogur - yogurt

Z

la zanahoria - carrot
el zapato - shoe
el zoológico - zoo